GCSE Double Award
Applied ICT
The Study Guide

This book takes you through everything you
need to know for GCSE Applied ICT.

For each unit, it's got plenty of
handy advice for doing the assessment.

If you're after a book for Applied ICT — this is it.

Contents

UNIT THREE — ICT AND SOCIETY

ASSESSMENT ADVICE

Published by Coordination Group Publications Ltd.

Contributors:
Steve Hacker
Dominic Hall
Simon Little
Phil Miles
Kate Redmond
Rachel Selway
David Smailes
Jennifer Underwood

With thanks to Sonia Stuart, Samantha Mc Sheffrey and Michelle Walters
for the proofreading.

ISBN: 1 84146 348 5

Groovy website: www.cgpbooks.co.uk

Jolly bits of clipart from CorelDRAW

Printed by Elanders Hindson, Newcastle upon Tyne.

Word Processing — Basics

Applied ICT is broken into 3 units (called "Teaching Modules" if you're doing OCR). The first unit, "ICT Tools and Applications", is covered in sections 1.1 to 1.4 of this book. For this unit, you need to know the <u>features</u> of different types of software and <u>how</u> to use them. First up, <u>word processors</u>...

Highlight *text you want to Edit*

You're <u>never</u> going to write something that's <u>perfect</u> first time. So you need to know the different ways to <u>edit</u> what you've written. For most changes, you need to <u>highlight</u> (select) the text first:

Highlighting text with the mouse:

1) <u>Double click</u> to select a word.
 ...orse, out came the cabbage.

2) <u>Click and drag</u> with the mouse to select exactly what you want.
 ...g, expanding into unexplored territor... ...ng pop and looked down in horror.

3) <u>Triple click</u> to select a whole paragraph.
 Just when I thought things couldn't get worse, she brought out the cabbage. I knew I would be sick soon. I could feel my stomach swelling, expanding into unexplored territory. Suddenly, I heard something pop and looked down in horror.

Highlighting text with the keyboard:

Hold down <u>shift</u> while you move the text cursor with the <u>cursor keys</u>.

Hold down <u>ctrl</u> as well to select a word at a time.

There are Four Ways to *Edit Text*

1) **DELETE** text. Use the <u>backspace</u> key to delete one character at a time. To delete a chunk of text, <u>highlight it</u> and press the backspace key.

2) **INSERT** and **REPLACE** text.
 To insert text, just click the cursor where you want it and start typing.
 To replace words or chunks of text, <u>highlight</u> the text you want to replace and start typing.

3) **MOVE** text using <u>cut and paste</u> or by <u>highlighting</u> and <u>dragging</u> it.

4) **REPEAT** text using <u>copy and paste</u>.

I must not make inappropriate noises or smells in class.

I must not make inappropriate noises or smells in class.
I must not make inappropriate noises or smells in class.
I must not make inappropriate noises or smells in class.
I must not make inappropriate noises or smells in class.
I must not make inappropriate noises or smells in class.
I must not make inappropriate noises or smells in class.

SOME EXTREMELY USEFUL KEYBOARD SHORTCUTS

CUT — CTRL X
COPY — CTRL C
PASTE — CTRL V
UNDO — CTRL Z

<u>Cut and paste</u> and <u>copy and paste</u> work in all programs, not just word processors. You'll use them <u>all the time</u> so learn these <u>keyboard shortcuts</u> for them.

<u>Undo</u> is another extremely handy one.

A nice easy start...

There's nothing too advanced on this first page. But it's all really important stuff, so make sure you learn it all. These basic <u>text editing</u> tricks work in most software applications, not just word processors. You'll save yourself loads of time later on if you learn them <u>now</u>.

Word Processing — Basics

Once you've got the words right, there's lots you can do to jazz up the appearance.

Four ways to Change the Look of your Text

1) **CHANGE THE FONT** Font is the fancy name for the style of the letters.
You need to choose one which matches the tone of the document you're producing.

Fish finger   Fish finger   Fish Finger   Ꮆꭵꮪꮒ ꭼꭵꮹꬽꭱ   **Fish finger** ← I wouldn't recommend this one — it's vile. Urrghh.

2) **CHANGE THE TEXT SIZE** Emphasise headings and subheadings by making them larger.
A font size between 10 and 12 point is easy to read for most people (this text is in 12 pt).
But small children and people with reading difficulties might need a larger font size.

3) **HIGHLIGHT THE TEXT** to make it stand out. There are four ways to do this:
(i) **bold type**, (ii) *italics,* (iii) underlined, (iv) colour.

4) **BULLETS AND NUMBERING** can be added for lists and key points. The computer automatically does the numbers or bullets each time you press enter until you tell it to stop.

Three ways you can Position your Text

1. **INDENTING** Use the tab key to indent a line of text. Or you can indent whole paragraphs to make them stand out.

2. **ALIGNING AND JUSTIFYING**

Text is usually left-aligned like this text here. Bla bla bla bla blab lab lablab bla bla. Bla bla bla bla bla bla bla bla.

This text is right-aligned. Right-aligned text is sometimes used for addresses at the top of letters.

This text is centre-aligned. Bla bla bla bla blabla blbalblbla. bla bla bla blblbla bla bla burp bla bla. a bla blblbla bla bla bla bla.

This text is justified which means that each full line is exactly the same length. Bla bloo bloap bling bla.

3. **LINE SPACING** Line spacing adjusts how far apart the lines of text are. Double-line spacing is much easier to read than single-line spacing — but it uses up much more paper.

Use the Formatting Toolbar

All decent word processors have a formatting toolbar like this.
Almost all the formatting you'll need to do can be done from here.

FONT   **TEXT SIZE**   **TEXT HIGHLIGHTING — BOLD, ITALIC AND UNDERLINE**   **COLOURS AND BORDERS**

| Heading 2 | Times New Roman | 12 | **B** *I* U | ≡ ≡ ≡ ≡ | ≣ ≣ ≇ ≇ | □ ▾ ✎ ▾ A |

PARAGRAPH STYLES   **ALIGNING AND TEXT JUSTIFICATION**   **BULLETS, NUMBERING AND INDENT.**

One for me, one for Matt, one for me, one format...

Make sure you really get to grips with the formatting toolbar and learn what all the different buttons are for. Most software applications you'll use will have similar toolbars with many buttons the same.

Word Processing — Basics

Most of the things on this page should also be pretty familiar —
but they are all ways of making a document look more <u>professional</u> and <u>readable</u>.

Tables and Columns can Help Readability

1) <u>Tables</u> are a good way to present <u>lists</u> of numerical or textual information, e.g. lists of names and addresses.

2) <u>Columns</u> can be created so that the text flows down the page and jumps automatically to the next column. This is great for newsletters and newspapers.

Choose the Correct Page Set-Up

Choosing the <u>page set-up</u> means deciding how the page will look when it has been printed. There are two main things to decide.

Portrait

Landscape

1) The layout can be either <u>portrait</u> (tall and narrow) or <u>landscape</u> (short and wide).

> (With A3, A4, A5 etc., A3 is 2x as big as A4, A4 is 2x as big as A5, and so on...)

2) The <u>size</u> of the paper you want to print on. The page can be A4 (the size of this book), bigger (e.g. A3), or smaller (e.g. A5 or business card size). However it is important to have the right size paper — and most printers can't print bigger than A4.

Watch Out for Widows and Orphans

<u>Orphans</u> are small blocks of text that don't quite fit onto the bottom of one page, and so get put on a new one. (<u>Widows</u> are the blocks of text they get separated from.) As well as looking <u>unprofessional</u>, they waste paper. There are two main ways of getting rid of widows and orphans.

1) <u>Reduce</u> the font size of the <u>entire text</u> so it fits onto a whole page (but not too small to read).

2) Adjust the <u>margins</u> at the top and bottom of the page. However, a page can look <u>cluttered</u> if text is too close to the edge of the page.

A table helps readability — you can put your book on it...

It's a good idea to pay attention to the stuff on this page. It'll help you to produce <u>beautifully presented work</u>, with which you can amaze your friends and confound your enemies. Yay.

SECTION 1.1— WORD PROCESSING, DTP AND PRESENTATION SOFTWARE

Word Processing — The Trickier Stuff

These are the slightly <u>fancier</u> word processing tools — and they're a bit <u>more tricky</u>.

Headers and Footers are Good for Multi-Page Documents

1) These are blocks of information at the <u>top</u> (<u>header</u>) or <u>bottom</u> (<u>footer</u>) of the page. They're especially useful in <u>multi-page</u> documents where similar information needs to be on each page.

2) The most common examples of information in a header or footer include: filename, title, date and page number. For example, each page can display that it is page X of a document Y pages long — and this is updated <u>automatically</u> if new pages are inserted.

HEADER

FOOTER

Find and Replace do Exactly What they Say...

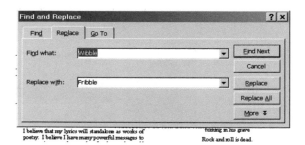

1) You can use <u>Find</u> to quickly locate a particular word in a document. It'll pick up occurrences of the word one at a time.

2) <u>Replace</u> does the same thing, but lets you swap it for a different word — either <u>individually</u> (with the "Replace" button) or <u>every time</u> it occurs (using "Replace All").

Mind Your Language with Spell- and Grammar-Checking

Most word processors can automatically correct your <u>spelling</u> and <u>grammar</u>.
This should improve the quality of your written communication — but there are <u>problems</u>.

SPELL-CHECKERS:

1) They come in different <u>languages</u>. Many words are spelt differently in different parts of the English speaking world — e.g. labor (American English) and labour (UK English). So if you live in the UK, check that you're using <u>UK English</u>.

2) They only recognise misspelt words — not their <u>context</u>. This is a problem with words like 'were' and 'where'. If you use the wrong one, the spell-checker won't find a problem.

3) Sometimes the dictionaries <u>contain</u> mistakes. One well-known word processor's spell-checker contained a <u>misspelling</u> of 'liaise'. (This is an example of 'garbage in garbage out'.)

GRAMMAR-CHECKERS:

Grammar-checkers can be <u>unreliable</u> and give confusing advice. This is because good grammar depends upon <u>context</u> — and most software isn't yet powerful enough to take this into account.

You can set Microsoft Word to check spelling and grammar as you go along. It underlines spelling mistakes in red and grammar mistakes in green.

I done a grammer and spell-checks on this page...

Lots of exciting wordprocessing features here — make sure <u>you can do</u> all the things on this page.

Word Processing — The Trickier Stuff

Now it's time to look at some really clever stuff.

Create Templates of Standard Documents

1) A template is a standard document containing pre-set formats and layouts. Their main benefit is that once they've been created, they save time — so they're often used for business letters.

2) A letter template contains spaces for the recipient's name, address, and the date. These are already formatted — the user just has to stick in the text.

Use Word Count to check how much you've written

1) Sometimes it's really handy to know how many words you've written, e.g. if you've got to do a 2000 word piece of coursework. Word processors have a word count feature to save counting the long way.

2) You can use it to count the words in your whole document, or in a chunk of text you've selected.

3) As well as giving you the number of words, it'll also tell you things like the number of paragraphs and lines in your document.

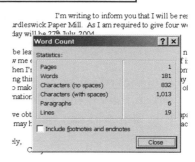

Import Information from Other Applications

1) Importing means adding data created using a different software application. A good example is the use of clip-art.

2) In order for imported data to work it must have been saved using a common file format that both pieces of software can recognise.

3) It's sometimes possible to embed a spreadsheet into a word-processed document and then activate it from within the word processor. Or you can link the spreadsheet to the document so that when the spreadsheet is edited, the word-processed document is automatically updated.

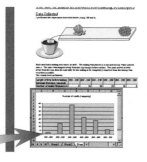

Linking works with other programs as well — not just spreadsheets and databases.

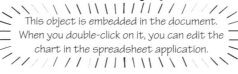
This object is embedded in the document. When you double-click on it, you can edit the chart in the spreadsheet application.

Use Macros to run Routine Operations

A macro is another time-saving device — and they're much simpler than most people think.

1) A macro is a sequence of commands that have been recorded by the computer and saved, using a short code as a filename. You run the macro by keying in the code — easy.

2) A good example is a macro to insert a footer containing the filename, date and page number into all new documents. Pretty nifty, you have to admit.

I'd rather have my routine operations done by a surgeon...

All these clever features are used by businesses to create fancy business documents like memos and invoices. Each business document will have its own template. The template will contain the imported company logo, headers and footers with the company details. Really clever ones might use macros.

Word Processing — Mail-Merge

Mail-merge is a really important tool for businesses. You create a standard letter for a particular purpose, e.g. a reminder letter, then can <u>automatically personalise</u> it for everyone you send it to.

There's Three Basics Steps To Doing a Mail-Merge

Here is the basic procedure...

1) A <u>database table</u> is created containing the information you want to appear in the personalised letter. (Instead of a database, you could also use a spreadsheet or a table in a word document).

Title	Surname	First Name	Address	Town	Postcode	Car	MOT Due
Mrs	Barnes	Clair	101 Brakespeare Avenue	Shepton Mallet	BN2 0JQ	M632 WMO	2nd March
Miss	Jones	Brenda	14 Church Street	Bath	BA1 HP3	W324 SLH	1st March
Mrs	Brake	Kate	34 Moorland Road	Swindon	SNT 5YU	ELV 15	23rd March
Miss	Duffy	Rachael	90 Browns Drive	Iceland	S64 JKL	RR1	17th March
Mr	Philips	Ben	25 High Road	Bath	SN5 TH9	WPO3 C6P	2nd March
Mr	Smith	Paul	23 New Road	Frome	SKI 90E	T604 HFN	30th March
Mrs	Stanley	Nigel	4 Robins Close	Dursley	BS4 5HP	CAH 007	11th March

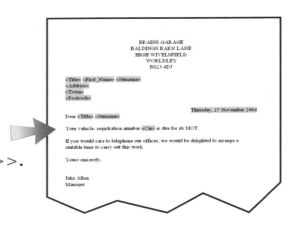

2) A <u>standard letter</u> is created containing codes which match the field names in the database. E.g. the address field appears as <<Address>>.

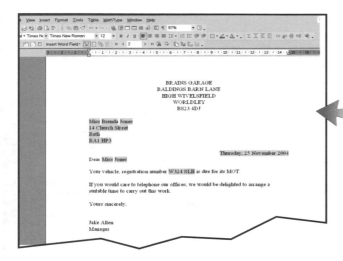

3) The standard letter is linked to the database. The software <u>merges</u> the data by inserting each database record in turn into the letter. If there are 1000 names in the database then you'll get 1000 personalised letters — and each one will greet the reader by their <u>surname</u>.

Most of the Post You Receive is Probably Mail-Merge

Most post (including <u>junk mail</u>) is produced by mail merge.

This table gives just a few examples.

Type of Letter	Personalised Details Needed
Gas or electricity bill	Name and address, Customer Number, Amount to Pay, Payment due date.
MOT reminder letter	Name and address, Car Registration, Car Make and Model
Bank statement	Name and address, Account number, Account name, transaction details
Exam Results Certificate	Name, Exam entry number, exam taken, grade awarded

Thank you mail-merge for bringing us junk mail...

Businesses use mail-merge <u>all the time</u> these days. It's much nicer to receive a letter personally addressed to you than one which says "Dear Sir / Madam". It feels like the letter's been written especially for <u>you</u>, but in actual fact it's also been sent to 10,000 other people...

Graphics — Capturing Images

Over the next three pages, we'll cover all the basic things you can do with graphic images — different ways to <u>create</u> them and ways to <u>manipulate</u> them. It's all useful stuff, so <u>pay attention</u>...

Images are Stored as either *Bitmap* or *Vector* Data

There are two types of graphics software. The main differences are to do with how they store the image, and how the image is edited.

A pixel is a coloured dot, and it can take thousands of dots to make up a whole picture.

PAINTING SOFTWARE (also known as <u>pixel-based</u> software)

1) The graphic is saved as a series of coloured dots (<u>pixels</u>) in a file called a <u>bitmap</u>. These files are large — each dot would be saved <u>individually</u>.

2) To edit the image, you basically alter each dot individually, although there are lots of different tools to make this easier.

Go on, admit it — you've been doctoring my image...

DRAWING SOFTWARE (also called <u>object-based</u> or <u>vector-based</u> software)

1) The image is saved as <u>coordinates</u> and <u>equations</u> *(e.g. a red circle might be represented by its radius, the coordinates of its centre and a number for its colour)* — making file sizes a lot smaller.

2) The image is edited by manipulating objects (e.g. squares, circles). You can stretch them, twist them, colour them and so on with a series of tools.

You can use Clip-Art...

1) <u>Clip-art</u> is graphics that have been created by someone else, but made available for you to copy. Some come <u>free</u> with software packages — others can be <u>bought</u> on CD-ROM.

2) It's possible to treat the <u>Internet</u> as a free clip-art source and <u>copy</u> graphics from web sites. But lots of images are protected by <u>copyright</u> — so using them without permission can be <u>illegal</u>.

...Input Existing Images...

Existing images (e.g. photographs) can be converted and stored as a <u>digital</u> image (i.e. data). There are two main ways to do this:

1) Photographs on film or in a book, or hand-drawings on paper need to be converted into a <u>digital</u> image using a <u>scanner</u>. These images are usually stored as <u>bitmap</u> files — so the files can be very large (though they can be converted to other formats, e.g. JPEGs).

Resolution means the number of pixels making up the image.

400 pixels | 50 pixels
400 pixels | 50 pixels

The more pixels used, the sharper the image — but the bigger the file.

A <u>JPEG</u> is a <u>compressed bitmap</u>. When you convert a bitmap to a JPEG, you <u>lose</u> some of the <u>picture quality</u>, but in a way that's <u>not noticeable</u> to the <u>human eye</u> — e.g. there might be slight colour changes. Compressing the image in this way can <u>massively reduce</u> the <u>file size</u>.

2) New images can be made using a <u>digital camera</u>, and then <u>downloaded</u> onto a computer. Digital photographs are initially stored as <u>JPEG</u> files — which are <u>usually</u> smaller than bitmaps, although the file size will depend on the level of resolution you've chosen.

...Or Create Your Own

<u>Creating</u> your own graphics by hand using the functions of the software can be very <u>time-consuming</u> — so it's often not worth doing unless there's <u>no</u> other way to get hold of the graphic you want.

Bad resolution — a broken promise on New Year's Day...

You need to be really familiar with all this <u>basic stuff</u>. If you're doing AQA, you'll need to use these skills to produce a company logo for your business documents (part of the unit 1 assessment). If you're doing Edexcel, you'll definitely need to import graphics as part of the unit 1 exam.

Graphics — Manipulating Images

Graphics software is changing rapidly — especially <u>image manipulation</u> software for digital photos. But whatever the technology, the same basic <u>principles</u> still apply. Learn what they are.

Resize the Object — But try not to Distort it

1) Resizing a graphic is often done after the image has been <u>exported</u> into a word processor or desktop-publishing package.

2) It's usually done by selecting the graphic and then dragging one of the '<u>handles</u>' — outwards to make the image bigger, and inwards to make it smaller.

handle

Something's not right...

3) The clever bit is to keep the <u>proportions</u> of the image the <u>same</u> — in other words to keep it the same shape. Otherwise the image gets <u>distorted</u> and it can look pretty bad. You'd be amazed at how many publications contain distorted images.

Cropping Removes Unwanted Bits

1) <u>Cropping</u> removes parts of the image you don't want — e.g. someone on the edge of the shot you want to get rid of. Cropping reduces the size of the image by removing blocks from the <u>edges</u> of the graphic.

2) It's a <u>quick</u> and <u>easy</u> way to remove bits of the image, although it can only remove whole <u>edges</u> — you can't use it to remove something in the <u>middle</u> of the graphic. Fortunately most graphics software has a separate tool to do this.

I think you cropped my head a bit too much.

Group Two or More Images Together

1) If you want to use an image that <u>isn't</u> in your clip-art library — for example a sheep riding a motorbike — but you <u>have</u> separate clip-art of a sheep and a motorbike, you can make a new object by <u>grouping</u> them together so that it looks like the sheep is riding the bike.

2) You can also select which graphics are at the <u>front</u> of the image and which are at the <u>back</u> — this is called <u>layering</u>.

Rotate and Recolour Objects

1) Images can be <u>rotated</u> to make them appear upside down, or <u>flipped</u> to appear back to front. Or you could make the Leaning Tower of Bradford by rotating an image just a little bit.

2) Images can also be <u>recoloured</u> — some packages will change the colour of the whole object automatically. With others you have to change it manually, pixel by pixel using a <u>paint spray</u>.

Learn the art of cropping — and be a cut above the rest...

There are some <u>extremely powerful</u> graphics packages around now, which give you some really <u>flash</u> effects (if you've got a few days spare to teach yourself, that is). But if you're just making a poster for the school fête, you can probably get away with something a bit more <u>straightforward</u>.

Graphics — Manipulating Images

With painting programs like Adobe Photoshop and Corel Photopaint, you can edit photos in all sorts of weird and wonderful ways that you wouldn't have thought possible.

Adjust the Brightness, Contrast and Sharpness

Most of the time your photos won't need anything too fancy doing to them. But sometimes a scanned-in photo might be too dark, or a photo from a digital camera might look a bit blurry.

You can easily sort these out by adjusting the brightness, contrast and sharpness.

Filters let you produce Funky Effects

Any decent painting package will come equipped with a range of weird filters that let you change the overall look of the image. Here are just a few of them in action.

My pet caterpillar, JLo.

Original image

Distort filter

Plastic wrap filter

Stained Glass filter

Charcoal filter

Hue determines the colours

Altering the Hue value changes the colours used in the image. These groovy images of JLo were made simply by changing the Hue value.

Stick Parts of Images together to make Fake Photos

You can also use painting software to do some great image-doctoring. It's quite fiddly at first, but with a bit of practice, you can create some great fake pictures.

Here's a photo I took of Britney the hippo driving my car. Ha ha fooled you... it's not real. I created it using Photoshop.

First, I drew round Britney with a SELECTION TOOL and created a COPY of that part of the image. Then I stuck Britney onto the image of my car.

Britney is on a different LAYER from the car, which means I can move and resize her without affecting the car image. The windscreen is also on a separate transparent layer in front of Britney.

Now you can create your own special photos of Britney...

Let's face it, as far as ICT topics go, this is one of the best. I mean, putting hippos in motorcars — it doesn't get any better than this. You need to have a play with the graphics software you have and see if you can do all the things shown on this page. (It doesn't have to involve hippos).

Desktop Publishing — Basics

Most of the stuff I said about word processing is relevant to <u>desktop publishing</u> (<u>DTP</u>) as well. But you also need to know how DTP is <u>different</u> from word processing.

DTP Creates Professional Looking Pages

1) <u>Desktop publishing</u> software is used to build <u>professional</u> looking pages — ones that are good enough to be <u>published</u>. Rather like this one (ahem).

Oh, and Brother John... I need 2,000 church newsletters by tomorrow as well...

2) Examples of documents produced using DTP software include newsletters, newspapers, leaflets and posters. But there are loads of others as well.

3) Pages are built up as a series of <u>frames</u> — <u>text frames</u> containing text, <u>graphics frames</u> containing images and so on.

4) DTP software usually lets the user create text and simple pictures — but it often works <u>best</u> when the source material is created in other <u>specialised</u> software (e.g. a word processor or a graphics package) and then <u>imported</u> into the DTP package.

DTP Software is usually Frame-Based

1) Frame-based software means that information is put on pages in <u>blocks</u> (called <u>frames</u>).

2) Frames can be <u>moved</u> or <u>resized</u>. This means that it is very easy to <u>edit</u> a DTP document by moving pictures or blocks of text around. Frames can also be moved from page to page.

3) DTP works rather like creating a <u>noticeboard</u> — you have a set of different pieces of information which you can move around until you're happy with the overall layout.

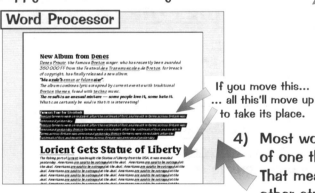

Each block of text or picture forms its own frame that you can drag around separately.

If you move this...
... all this'll move up to take its place.

4) Most word processors are <u>not</u> frame-based, so the position of one thing depends on the position of everything else. That means moving one thing might make a whole load of other stuff move as well. This doesn't happen with DTP.

(cos it's ace)

DTP has Three Main Benefits

1) You can create very <u>professional-looking</u> documents — even with relatively <u>inexpensive</u> DTP packages. But the quality of the printed document is often limited by the quality of the <u>printer</u>.

2) The <u>layout</u> of the document can be changed more easily using DTP than a word processor.

3) The user can control the number of pages more easily than when using a word processor. If there are too many words for a page in a word processor, it will normally create a new page automatically — however the DTP software will usually just not display the text.

DTP — what can you say.... hmmm....DTP...   yep...

Lots of people think they're <u>experts</u> at <u>DTP</u> — but it's <u>easy</u> to make a <u>mess</u> of it. Remember, it's not just having the <u>skills</u> — you need to think about your document's <u>purpose</u> too.

Desktop Publishing — Basics

It's the <u>frames</u> that really make <u>DTP</u> software <u>more powerful</u> than a word processor for some tasks. You need to be aware of how <u>frames</u> and <u>templates</u> can <u>improve the layout</u> of a document. ☺

Four Things You can do with a Frame

1) Frames can be lined up in <u>columns</u> — most DTP software can insert <u>column guides</u> or <u>guidelines</u> (lines that appear on <u>screen</u> but not on the printed document) to help position the frames. This keeps the document looking tidy, and the layout <u>consistent</u>.

2) Text frames can be <u>linked</u> together, so any text not fitting inside the first text frame will automatically appear inside the next one. Frames can even be linked across different pages of the document — so they're handy if you want to continue a story on a different page.

3) If a picture frame is positioned on top of a text frame you can set the text to <u>wrap around</u> a picture, instead of being covered by it.

The dotted line around the picture shows it's set to wrap text around it.

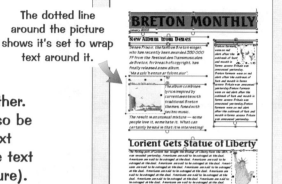

4) Frames can be <u>layered</u> — i.e. put on top of each other. This is usually done with picture frames, but can also be done with text frames. E.g. you could put some text over the top of a picture (but you have to make the text frame transparent first so you can still see the picture).

Templates Save Time Designing Pages

1) The <u>Golden Rule</u> of good page design in DTP is keep the page layout <u>simple</u>, and <u>appropriate</u> for the needs of the audience. Templates can make this easier.

2) <u>Templates</u> are files containing the basic <u>layout</u> and <u>format</u> for a standard document. Most DTP software has loads of different templates. They save time but if you're not careful, documents can end up looking the same.

Text box to insert date.

Title already formatted.

Text and picture frames and column guidelines (or guides) already set up.

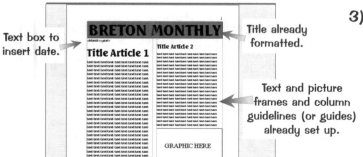

3) A template for a newspaper will have <u>columns</u>, <u>text frames</u> and <u>picture frames</u>. The text frames will be formatted with different fonts for the newspaper title, headlines and main story.

4) Templates can also be designed by the user — e.g. for a <u>school newsletter</u>. At the top of the template's first page would be the school name, address, crest, and a <u>text box</u> for the date. The basic <u>layout</u> of the other pages may also be set — e.g. a page for PE results might contain graphics to represent the main sports, and tables where results can be entered.

DTP — get yourself in the right frame of mind...

Desktop publishing's not too difficult. Getting your pages looking pretty can even be quite good <u>fun</u>. It's not <u>just</u> about looking nice though — your DTP pages should be designed with your <u>target audience</u> in mind, and should be <u>carefully planned</u> so that it appeals to them.

Desktop Publishing — Newsletters

One of the common uses of DTP that you should know about is creating <u>newsletters</u>.
For businesses, they're a good way of informing customers of <u>new products</u> and <u>sales promotions</u>.

Newsletters Grab our Attention with their Layout

A good newsletter will use various layout and style features to make it look interesting and attractive.

COMPANY LOGO
All material from the company will have the logo clearly displayed in a familiar visual style — this helps to promote the company's brand.

MAIN TITLE
The main title is always in a big, bold font that shouts the message out in a few short words.

GRAPHICS
These are usually colourful and clear pictures that back up what's in the articles.

December 2003

JJ PC

JJPC what's new?

Christmas is coming!
Just look at our prices!

Thinking of buying a new PC for Christmas? At JJPC we have a number of top quality, lightning fast machines at affordable prices, ready for immediate delivery. Our Pentium 4 Tandem features the latest Voodoo graphics card PLUS a DVD burner, all for an unbelievable JJPC price of £499. Add just £80 and get a huge 18" TFT flat screen bundled with your system. Hurry, as we expect these to fly out of the store!

If mobility is your thing, we also have a mobile Pentium 4 laptop, with a free carry case, a 54G wireless adaptor and three year warranty for a seasonal price of £799.

New Technical Manager

Many JJPC regulars have already met Herm, our new technical director, who joins us from Dell.

Formerly a technical manager at Dell, Herm has been involved in large scale product development for the past 7 years, before which he studied for a Phd in computer software engineering at Imperial College, London. Herm says that he is looking forward to working with the JJPC team, and introducing some of the latest technologies.

HEADINGS
These sum up what the text below is about — they make it easier to skim through and pick out the bits that interest you. Experiment with STYLES in your DTP program to get the best effect.

BODY TEXT
The main text is arranged in columns.

SHORT ARTICLES
Company newsletters are usually a way of advertising products or services — articles are kept short to maintain interest.

TEXT STYLES
Different parts of the newsletter use different fonts, sizes, colours and formatting. These are all chosen to match the tone of the document and so they complement each other. You can set up paragraph styles in the DTP program to automatically format the different types of text.

A company newsletter like this would have its own <u>template</u> with the basic layout and paragraph styles already set up. When it's time to produce a new newsletter, all the text and graphics would just be <u>pasted in</u> to the template. It's then easy to <u>tweak</u> the layout to finish it.

House Style sets the Rules on How Documents Look

Every company has its own <u>house style</u> — the set of design and writing <u>rules</u> all its team follow. The house style is tailored to suit the newsletter's <u>audience</u>. It includes things like the kind of <u>layout</u> and <u>fonts</u> you choose and <u>the way you write</u> — whether you use simple or long words and sentences. The house style also decides whether you write in a formal or a chatty tone.

House Style — sounds like a job for Bowen and Smiley...

Having a distinct house style helps a company to develop a <u>strong brand</u>. With a really good house style, you'll be able to <u>recognise</u> the company from the document style alone — this applies to adverts, newsletters, letters, leaflets, everything a company might print on paper.

Multimedia Presentations — Basics

Presentation software is being used more and more to give talks and display ideas. You need to know what it is suitable for and what the main features are.

Presentations are used to Communicate New Information

1) Presentations are given to communicate information to a group of people. A teacher might give a presentation to introduce a new topic in a lesson, or a salesperson could give one to persuade people to buy something.

2) They can sometimes be quite boring — especially if the speaker just talks on and on. Presentation software can help overcome this by using multimedia and animation effects.

Presentations can be given With or Without a Speaker

1) The typical way to give a presentation is with a speaker introducing slides projected onto a large screen. The audience can read the information on the screen while the speaker gives them more detailed spoken information.

2) The other way is to give a presentation without a speaker. For this to work well the slides have to be good enough to communicate all the required information by themselves. Multimedia presentation software can help by allowing a commentary to be recorded.

Presentation Software has Four Main Features

1) Presentation software creates a series of slides in a single document — and each slide contains a number of frames (a bit like DTP software). This means that text and images — and even movies and sounds — can be put on the slide.

2) The really clever thing about presentation software is that the speaker can decide when each frame on a page appears — so each bullet point in a list can appear on screen at just the right moment.

3) Animation effects can even make the frames arrive on screen in different ways. (See page 15.)

4) The animation effects can either happen at set times (useful if there's no speaker), or they can be controlled by the speaker as he/she is talking — usually with the click of a mouse or a remote control button.

How Presentations used to be Done

1) Traditionally slides were either handwritten or word-processed.

2) Unfortunately, it's easy to muddle up the order of the slides.

3) Another problem is that the speaker sometimes has to cover up information they don't want the audience to see yet.

4) Unless the speaker's very good, a presentation can easily end up looking unprofessional.

If you only learn one thing about presentations, learn this...

Here is a REALLY useful tip for using presentation software. I'm going to deliver it "flying bulletpoint" style. Ready...

• ALWAYS CA

Multimedia Presentations — Creating One

Creating multimedia presentations requires you to <u>plan</u> out the presentation, <u>collect</u> data and multimedia elements, <u>build</u> the presentation, <u>test it</u> and then <u>use</u> it. Aren't you lucky?

It Helps to Plan Your Presentation Properly

It's really important to <u>plan</u> your presentation properly, or it'll end up looking pretty shonky. When you're planning, make sure you think about these things:

- What the <u>purpose</u> of the presentation is.
- What <u>information</u> it needs to get across.
- How you want to <u>organise</u> the content and order of the slides.
- How it's going to be <u>used</u>, and by who.

There are two ways of planning your presentation:

Make a <u>STORYBOARD</u> — Sketch out a series of boxes showing how you want each <u>page</u> to look, and what elements you might want to include.

> Main title
>
> introduction — about us, where we are...
>
> logo →
>
> ☐ home button
> *Note - plain transition to next slide, play theme on slide open*

Make a <u>STRUCTURE DIAGRAM</u> — Draw a <u>plan</u> to show how slides will <u>link</u> together. It could be one slide after the other, or hierarchical like the one below.

> Start page
> Product range | Recent sales | Future plans
> Good stuff | Rubbish stuff

Once you've completed your planning, you're ready to <u>build</u> your presentation.

Use the Slide Master to Create Your Basic Slide Layout

'<u>Slide Master</u>' is, surprise surprise, a <u>master slide</u>. It lets you make changes to the <u>basic</u> slide <u>layout</u>. These changes appear in all the other slides. This helps to give a <u>consistent</u> feel to the presentation.

1) You can change the <u>fonts</u> and <u>background</u> that'll be used for all your slides.
2) You can even make changes to the <u>standard</u> slide design <u>templates</u>.
3) You can add common elements like <u>images</u> that will appear on every slide (which is useful for adding a '<u>home</u>' link).

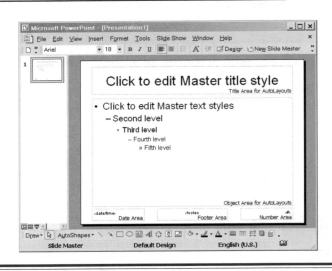

If you only learn one other thing, learn this...

To get to the Slide Master in Powerpoint, click on 'View', then 'Master', then 'Slide Master'. <u>Easy</u>.

Multimedia Presentations — Creating One

Here's how to do all those fiddly little things that'll make your presentation look really <u>professional</u>.

Add Navigation to Get From Slide to Slide

Your slides will <u>automatically</u> run in order in your slide show, but if you want to do anything more <u>complicated</u>, you need to add some <u>navigation</u>. There are two ways to do this.

1) Adding <u>action buttons</u> to your slides — these are buttons to go back, forward, home or to a slide of your choice.

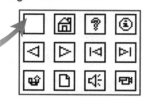

> In Powerpoint, click on 'Slide Show', then 'Action buttons', to see a choice of buttons. Click on the one you want, then click on your slide to place the button.

2) Using <u>hyperlinks</u> — just like adding <u>links</u> to web pages in a web site, you can add links to slides in a presentation. They can be added to graphics, text or selected bits of images ('hotspots').

> To add a link in Powerpoint, highlight what you want to use as a hyperlink and go to 'Insert' then 'Hyperlink' then 'Bookmark'. Select the slide you want to hyperlink to then click OK.

So when you're giving your presentation, <u>just click</u> on the button or hyperlink to go to the right slide.

Animation Effects are Quite Cool

There are loads of things you can do with <u>animation effects</u>. You can make your frame bounce into place, whizz on with a 'ping' or swirl about like a mad thing.

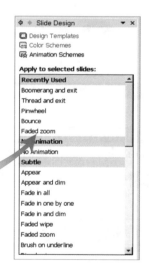

> In Powerpoint, go to 'Animation schemes' and you'll get a list of exciting animations to choose from. Don't overdo it though — overanimation can look a wee bit ridiculous.

Add Multimedia if You're a Show Off

Powerpoint comes with certain <u>sounds</u> you can use — like boingy and swishy noises for when you change slides, and applause for when you're feeling a bit big-headed. They can be useful sometimes, but can get <u>annoying</u> after a while.

1) You can add your <u>own sounds</u>, if you like, which is normally much more useful.
2) Just insert a <u>hyperlink</u>, but instead of linking it to a slide, link it to a <u>sound file</u> on your computer.
3) You can <u>play</u> the sound by clicking on the hyperlink. Amazing.
4) You can add <u>video</u> in exactly the same way, and it looks **REALLY** professional.

AnimAnimAnimAnimation...weeee!

Here's a fairly useful tip... save your presentation as a PowerPoint show (.pps) — then when you double click on the file it will <u>launch directly</u> into the show. (Which looks quite professional.)

Multimedia Presentations — Handy Tips

It's one thing to have clever software to produce exciting slides — but it's another thing to know how to use the software to produce a good presentation. Make sure you learn the following rules.

Remember the Rules for Giving a Good Presentation

1) **PREPARE THOROUGHLY** — make sure you know all about the topic you're presenting. The whole point is to get people interested enough that they'll want to ask questions — so you need to have all the answers.

2) **DECIDE ON THE FORMAT** for the presentation — decide whether you'll be delivering it in person, or making it available as a computer file.

3) **WRITE THE SCRIPT** of the presentation first — then decide how the slides will help put the key points of the message across. The slides should be a summary of the main points to be made.

4) **KEEP THE SLIDES SIMPLE** — don't let background colours clash with the text and pictures. Ideally use the same background for all the slides, and don't use hard-to-read fonts. Use no more than two pictures per slide.

5) **USE OPENING AND CLOSING SLIDES** — start the presentation with an attention-grabbing opening slide. The closing slide should leave people with the main message of the presentation.

6) **KEEP EACH SLIDE'S CONTENT TO A MINIMUM** — the Golden Rule is to have no more than six words per line of text and no more than five lines of text on a slide. Font sizes should be big enough for people at the back of the audience to see — between **30** and **60** point should do.

7) **DON'T USE TOO MANY SLIDES** — if you're giving a commentary, each slide should be visible for about two minutes. That means no more than five main slides in a ten-minute presentation.

8) **TEST ANY ANIMATION EFFECTS** using the hardware that will be used in the presentation. Large movie clips might run very slowly on some systems.

9) **REHEARSE** — then rehearse, then rehearse again.

Presentation Software has Pros and Cons

Funding the New
Presentation Software

One member of staff to go
(((No more tea or cof

ADVANTAGES OF USING PRESENTATION SOFTWARE

1) It produces professional looking presentations.

2) Use of multimedia can help grab and keep people's attention.

3) Presentations can be saved and used again — with or without the speaker being present.

4) It's easy to edit presentations and adapt them for different audiences.

DISADVANTAGES OF USING PRESENTATION SOFTWARE

1) It is very easy to get carried away by the technology and produce badly designed slides.

2) The software needs expensive hardware to run the presentation — a laptop computer and an LCD projector can easily cost over £3000.

Do a good presentation — don't make an exhibition of yourself...

This presentation software is really useful, but you need lots of practice to handle it properly.

Section 1.1 — Revision Summary

Phew, that's the first section over with. And quite a long one it was too. Before you continue, have a look through the questions below. They'll test whether or not you've remembered the stuff covered so far. Knowing and understanding what each type of software is for and what it can do is the first step, and then you need to make sure you can use it all...

1) Describe two ways to highlight the text you want to edit.

2) What do these shortcuts do?
    a) Ctrl x   b) Ctrl v   c) Ctrl c   d) Ctrl z

3) Explain how to move some text from one document to another.

4) How have the following words been formatted? (Use the correct words).
    a) **fish pie**   b) *fish pie*   c) <u>fish pie</u>

5) List as many ways as you can think of to make words stand out on a page.

6) What is the difference between left, right and centre alignment and justification?

7) Which is the bigger paper size: A4 or A5? How much bigger is it?

8) Why should you avoid having widows and orphans?

9) Name four things that a business document might have in a header.

10) Give one benefit and one problem of using a spell-checker.

11) Why is a common file format needed to import data from a graphics file into a word processor?

12) What is a template?

13) Explain how mail merge works.

14) Explain one benefit and one problem of mail merge.

15) What is the difference between pixel-based and vector-based graphics software?

16) Is drawing software pixel-based or vector-based?

17) How can a printed photograph be entered into a computer system?

18) Which type of image file is usually bigger — a bitmap or a JPEG?

19) Explain the difference between resizing and cropping an image.

20) What is the main difference between how pages are built up using word processing software and using DTP software?

21) Give two benefits of using DTP software over using word processing software.

22) Give three ways that newsletters should use layout to grab our attention.

23) What is house style? What are the benefits to a company of having a house style?

24) Give three advantages of using presentation software over traditional overhead projector slides for doing a presentation.

25) What two things could you produce to plan your presentation?

26) What is the 'slide master' for?

27) What are the two main ways of adding navigation to your presentation?

28) Give five guidelines for a good presentation. (No looking at the opposite page, you cheat.)

29) Are you ready to start Section 1.2?   a) Yes   b) Yes   c) Yes

Spreadsheets — Basics

Most people find spreadsheets a little bit scary — very few people really <u>understand</u> them. But they're basically pretty simple. Make sure you know this page well before moving onto the trickier stuff.

Spreadsheets are Clever Calculators

1) A spreadsheet is simply a program that can <u>display</u> and <u>process</u> data in a <u>structured</u> way. Most people think spreadsheets can only process <u>numbers</u> — but they can handle <u>text</u> as well.

2) Spreadsheets can be used to: a) <u>record</u> data,
   b) <u>search</u> for particular items of data,
   c) <u>perform calculations</u> based on data,
   d) produce <u>graphs</u> and <u>charts</u>.

3) <u>Examples</u> of uses include keeping records of patients in a doctor's surgery, calculating the exam results of a group of pupils, and producing graphs based on the results of a questionnaire.

Data is Entered into Cells

1) A spreadsheet is made up of <u>rows</u> and <u>columns</u>. These divide the sheet up into individual <u>cells</u>.

2) Each cell can be identified using the column letter and row number as <u>coordinates</u>.

Columns

Rows

The red cell is in Column B and Row 3 — so its cell reference is B3.

Each Cell can contain One of Three Things

Each cell can contain <u>one</u> (and only one) of three things...

NUMERICAL DATA	TEXT DATA	FORMULAS
e.g. numbers, dates and money. Most spreadsheets recognise dates and money and convert them into a suitable format — so if you enter 23-6, it's converted to 23 June.	e.g. people's names, titles of CDs. 1) Column headings usually contain text. 2) One process that can be carried out on text is sorting it into alphabetical order. 3) The ICT term for a piece of text is a <u>text string</u>.	1) These allow results of calculations to be displayed inside a cell. 2) E.g. you could get the computer to add up all the numbers in a column and display the answer in a cell at the bottom of the column. 3) The great thing about spreadsheets is that if any numbers are changed, the formulas are automatically updated.

The <u>Golden Rule</u> is to put only one piece of data in a cell — this means that you shouldn't <u>mix</u> any of these types of data.

1) If you enter the weight of a kilo of fish as '1000g' then you have <u>numerical</u> data (1000) and <u>text</u> data (g).

2) Spreadsheets treat cells with any text in them as though they contain <u>only</u> text data, which has a numerical value of <u>zero</u>.

3) This means the spreadsheet will read '1000g' as having a numerical value of <u>zero</u>. Bummer.

Most spreadsheets let you lock cells when you've entered your data, so it can't be changed. You have to choose 'Protect sheet' in the Tools menu as well though, or it won't work.

The exceptions are things like currencies where the spreadsheet knows that £5 has a value of 5.

Take a recess — and learn about cells...

The best way to get to grips with spreadsheets (or any new kind of software) is to go and have a <u>play</u> with them. That goes for the rest of this section. Once you've read a page, go and try out the stuff you've learnt <u>on a computer</u>. You might even enjoy it.

Spreadsheets — Basics

Spreadsheets are used to <u>process</u> data and then <u>communicate</u> the information.
That means it's important to know how to set up a spreadsheet properly.

Three Ways to <u>Improve the Design</u> of a Spreadsheet...

1) Put the <u>title</u> of the spreadsheet at the <u>top</u> — normally in cell <u>A1</u>.
   - If the title's too big to fit in A1, it'll spill into cells A2, A3 etc. — this <u>isn't</u> a problem.
   - If a spreadsheet's going to be used as the <u>data file</u> for a mail merge,
     the first row has to contain <u>field names</u> — so put the title into a <u>header</u>.

2) Next enter the <u>column</u> and <u>row headings</u>.
   - Don't leave any columns or rows <u>empty</u> — they cause problems with <u>charts</u> and <u>graphs</u>.
   - Increase the column <u>width</u> if necessary.

3) Enter <u>data</u> into the cells.
   - Change the cells' <u>format</u> to show numbers
     to a certain number of <u>decimal places</u>, or
     with a <u>currency</u> symbol if it's money.
   - Most spreadsheets let you use data
     <u>validation</u> formulas — so if you put an
     age as 1290, you get an error message.

	A	B	C
1	Mike's Musical Instrument Shop — Customer Accounts		
2	Customer Name	Amount Paid to date	Amount Still Owing
3	Gillian Clarke	£70.00	£80.00
4	Matthew Miller	£0.00	£550.00
5	Prittih Patel	£115.00	£640.00
6	Joshua Scott	£430.00	£770.00
7	Nancy Westwood	£55.00	£20.00
8	Malika Dawson	£320.00	£230.00
9	Simon Chester	£25.00	£75.00

...and Three Ways to <u>Improve its Appearance</u>

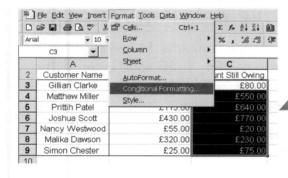

1) Format the data in similar ways to a <u>word processor</u>.
   Use <u>italics</u>, <u>bold</u>, different <u>fonts</u>, <u>colours</u>, <u>sizes</u> etc.
   to make data stand out.

2) Some spreadsheets allow <u>conditional formatting</u>.
   The format of a cell's changed if the contents of the cell
   meets certain <u>conditions</u> — e.g. you could choose to
   make the cells turn red if a person owed more than £100.

3) Some spreadsheets let you insert graphics, movies and
   sounds. This is quite a handy feature — probably.

Spreadsheet Data can be <u>Imported</u> <u>and</u> <u>Exported</u>

1) If the data you want to put in a spreadsheet is in another file somewhere else (like in a <u>database</u>
   or a <u>data-logging</u> device), you can <u>import</u> it directly into the spreadsheet — but only if the data is
   in a <u>common file format</u> such as <u>CSV</u>. This saves you the bother of typing it all in again.

2) CSV stands for <u>Comma-Separated Variable</u>. When the data is saved, a <u>comma</u> is inserted
   between each piece of data in a row, and a <u>line break</u> is inserted between the last piece of data in
   one row and the first in the next row. CSV data can be <u>transferred</u> easily between spreadsheets,
   tables and databases.

3) Integrated <u>software suites</u> that combine spreadsheets and word processors can transfer data
   between the applications by using <u>copy</u> and <u>paste</u>. This is simpler but is still based on CSV.

CSV Ltd. — an Import-Export Business...

If you don't know this stuff already, get yourself on a computer, load up a spreadsheet and try
<u>doing</u> all the things described on this page. It's all good <u>clean</u> fun.

Spreadsheets — Simple Formulas

Without formulas, spreadsheets are just fancy tables. They really put the <u>cool</u> into 'cool spreadsheet'.

A Formula is a Simple Computer Program

1) A <u>formula</u> is an instruction to the computer to <u>process</u> data held in specific cells — using <u>functions</u> which you can either type in or select from a list.

> STEP 1 — Click on the cell where you want the <u>answer</u>.
>
> STEP 2 — Type an <u>equals</u> sign (=).
>
> STEP 3 — Type in the <u>formula</u>. Here, it'd be <u>C3+D3+E3</u>.

The equals sign tells the computer to expect a formula.

	A	B	C	D	E	
	SUM	▼ × ✓ =	=C3+D3+E3			
1	Sales Team Performance					
2	First Name	Last name	Week 1 Sales	Week 2 Sales	Week 3 Sales	Total
3	Teresa	Wood	24	15	32	=C3+D3+E3
4	Tanya	Hide	33	30	41	
5	Colin	Moore	27	32	29	
6	Phillip	Farley	18	19	22	
7	Mia	Fernandez	35	33	26	

2) The simplest functions are +, −, * (for <u>multiply</u>) and / (for <u>divide</u>), but there are loads of others, e.g. <u>SUM</u> automatically totals a group of numbers or <u>AVERAGE</u> will calculate the mean.

3) Once you've entered a formula, you can <u>copy</u> it to other cells. So the formula in F3 could be copied to cells F4 to F7 — and the computer would automatically insert the correct formulas for the totals of these rows.

This makes spreadsheets an easy way to do lots of <u>similar</u> calculations on a <u>large</u> set of data.

Formulas can have <u>Absolute</u> or <u>Relative Cell References</u>

1) In the example above, the formula in F3 (=C3+D3+E3) tells the computer to add together the data in the three cells to the left. If you copy this formula to cell F4, it still adds together the contents of the three cells to the left, so F4 becomes '=C4+D4+E4'. That's why they're called relative cell references — the data used is in the same place <u>relative to the answer cell</u>.

2) Sometimes part of a formula always needs to refer to <u>one particular cell</u> — you don't want the computer to change the cell reference. Then you need to use an <u>absolute</u> cell reference — one that won't be changed. You do this by putting a dollar sign in front of the cell's coordinates. So B12 is a relative cell reference — but B12 is an absolute cell reference.

3) The spreadsheet below uses an absolute cell reference
(to represent the % commission a letting agency charges on its properties).

	A	B	C	D
1	Property	Monthly Rent	Letting Agent's commission	Amount to Landlord
2	Oak Vale	£450	£45	£405
3	The Old Post Office	£300	£30	£270
4	Ash House	£250	£25	£225
5	Lilac Cottage	£150	£15	£135
6	Low Wood	£500	£50	£450
7			£165	£1,485
8				
9	Letting Agent's Commission (%):		10	

Column C:
=B2 / 100 * C9
=B3 / 100 * C9
=B4 / 100 * C9
=B5 / 100 * C9
=B6 / 100 * C9

Column D:
=B2 − C2
=B3 − C3
=B4 − C4
=B5 − C5
=B6 − C6

Once you've entered the formula for C2, you can copy and paste it to cells C3 to C6 and it will automatically insert the correct formula.

Relative cell — we keep Granny in ours...

There's plenty of stuff here to learn. Make sure you're clear on how to enter and copy formulas. And as well as knowing the difference between <u>absolute</u> and <u>relative</u> cell references, it'd be handy if you knew a couple of examples of where you'd use each one.

Spreadsheets — The Trickier Stuff

If there's <u>something</u> you want to do with a spreadsheet, <u>chances are</u> there's a formula to do it. Which is handy. This stuff can seem tricky and quite scary at first, but when you've got your head round it you'll realise how much <u>time</u> and <u>effort</u> spreadsheets can save you.

Logic Functions let the Spreadsheet Decide What to Do

1) <u>Logic functions</u> do different things depending on the data in other cells — e.g. if the number in a cell containing a temperature is <u>negative</u>, the output of the logic function could be "Chilly", while if it's <u>positive</u>, the output could be "Warm".

2) In this spreadsheet, the <u>total sales</u> made by staff over three weeks are in column C. Sales people who made 80 sales or less are to be given extra training. The <u>logic function</u> in column D tells the spreadsheet to display the word "Yes" if the number in column C is 80 or less, and "No" if it's above 80.

	A	B	C	D
1	Sales Team Performance			
2	First Name	Last name	Total	Training?
3	Teresa	Wood	71	Yes
4	Tanya	Hide	104	No
5	Colin	Moore	88	No
6	Phillip	Farley	59	Yes
7	Mia	Fernandez	94	No

3) This uses the logic function <u>IF</u>. The output cell will display a specific output <u>if</u> a condition is met.

This formula is '=IF(C7>80,"No","Yes")' — meaning if the condition 'C7>80' is met, then display "No", otherwise display "Yes".

4) Logic functions can save a lot of <u>time</u>, and reduce the chances of <u>human error</u>.

IF (NOT D11<12 AND C5=2, "Rabbit", "Stew")

Thumper proves there's nothing quite as scary as logic functions.

Look-Up Tables Display Specified Data

1) A <u>look-up table</u> is a bit like a database. Data is stored in a table in one part of the spreadsheet, and in another part you can display data from that table.

2) Here, a shop selling vampire supplies has listed its products at the bottom of the spreadsheet. At the top, the user <u>enters</u> a <u>product code</u> into cell B1 — the spreadsheet then automatically displays the <u>product name</u> in B2 and the <u>price</u> in B3.

Enter a product code here...  ...and the details appear here.

	A	B	C
1	Product Code	26346	
2	Product Name	Garlic repellent	
3	Price	£0.50	
4			
5	Product Code	Product Name	Price
6	12532	Black capes	£25.99
7	65489	Sharp teeth	£5.50
8	26346	Garlic repellent	£0.50
9	57343	Sunglasses	£15.99
10	23908	Assorted bats	£25.99
11	31092	White face paint	£5.99
12	23412	Light meter	£34.50

3) The formulas in cells B2 and B3 are pretty scary — but basically they <u>search</u> the data in cells A6-A12, and display the data next to the relevant product code.

4) Look-up tables are pretty useless for small data sets like this one because you can just find the information yourself. But they're really useful for <u>large</u> data sets such as supermarket stocklists.

Look-up tables — but you won't like what you find...

You'll be <u>mainly</u> using <u>simpler</u> spreadsheets in your work for this Applied ICT GCSE, so it's not always easy to see the point of this tricky stuff. But exploring the ways that ICT is used in <u>different</u> <u>organisations</u> is quite important in the course, so try thinking about it from that point of view.

Spreadsheets — Graphs and Charts

Don't worry about the difference between graphs and charts
— basically they're just different ways of <u>communicating data</u> in visual form.

Creating a Chart is Dead Easy...

All modern spreadsheets can produce <u>graphs</u> and <u>charts</u> — but each one
uses a slightly different method. The basic idea is always the same though.

STEP ONE: Get all the data you want to put into a graph into a <u>single</u>
<u>block</u>. It's best if the data is arranged in <u>columns</u>.

STEP TWO: <u>Highlight</u> the data you want to use — you might need
to highlight the <u>column headings</u> as well.

STEP THREE: Select the <u>type</u> of chart you want — be sensible
and make sure it's <u>suitable</u>.

STEP FOUR: Choose a meaningful <u>title</u> for the chart, that
summarises its contents. <u>Label</u> any axes.

STEP FIVE: Decide if the chart needs a <u>key</u> (also called a <u>legend</u>).

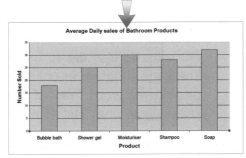

...but you need to know which ones are Appropriate

Spreadsheets can create so many different types of graph — but you need to choose the right kind.
Sometimes it's just a matter of <u>taste</u>, but sometimes there are definite <u>rights</u> and <u>wrongs</u>.

1) **BAR GRAPHS** display a <u>category</u> on the x-axis and a <u>value</u> on the
y-axis. Use a bar graph when each category is <u>discrete</u> (separate
from the others) — e.g. the number of a certain product sold.

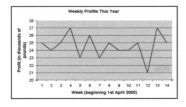

2) **LINE GRAPHS** are similar, but are used when the data on the x-axis
<u>isn't</u> in categories — like 'time' when you show the weekly profits
of a company over a period of several months.

3) **SCATTER GRAPHS** show the <u>relationship</u> between <u>two sets</u> of data —
plot one set along the x-axis and one set on the y-axis, and add a
<u>trend line</u> to show the relationship more clearly.

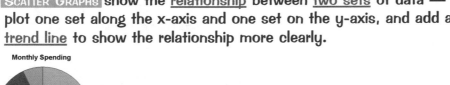

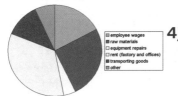

4) **PIE CHARTS** show the <u>contributions</u> of
categories to a <u>total</u> — e.g. a chart
showing what a company spent money on.

...the size of the cow's udder representing anticipated profits...

It's tempting to try to be too clever, and use <u>fancy</u> graphs that aren't really any
clearer than something <u>basic</u>. Again the golden rule is keep it simple — make sure
the graph gets its <u>point</u> across, and ideally <u>test</u> it by showing it to an intended user.

Pie-charts — I'd prefer pizza-charts myself...

Now, this is where spreadsheets <u>really</u> come in handy. Much easier to press a couple of buttons
and get your computer to make you a <u>beautiful graph</u> than it is sitting there for twenty minutes
with a ruler and pencil. Have a practise — it's really easy when you know how.

Databases — Introduction

Databases are really just convenient ways to store and manage lots of data. They're not just tables of info — there are all sorts of clever things you can do with them. Read on...

A Database is a Store of Data

1) A database is an <u>organised</u> collection of data which consists of one or more <u>tables</u> like this.

2) The information is split into <u>records</u> and <u>fields</u>.

3) The <u>columns</u> of the database table are the fields and each <u>row</u> is a different record.

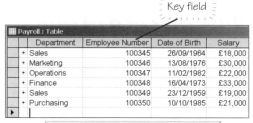

	Department	Employee Number	Date of Birth	Salary
+	Sales	100345	26/09/1964	£18,000
+	Marketing	100346	13/08/1976	£30,000
+	Operations	100347	11/02/1982	£22,000
+	Finance	100348	16/04/1973	£33,000
+	Sales	100349	23/12/1959	£19,000
+	Purchasing	100350	10/10/1985	£21,000

A simple payroll database table.

4) The <u>key field</u> contains an item of data that is <u>unique</u> to each record — so no records have the same value in the key field. Here, the employee number is the key field.

5) The big benefit of databases is that you can <u>search</u> them quickly to find specific data, or use them to generate <u>reports</u> — e.g. which books in a publisher's database have sold the most.

Well-Structured Fields are Really Important

1) The first step in creating a database is to decide on what <u>fields</u> you need. And once you've decided that, each field needs a <u>name</u>, a <u>description</u> of its contents, a <u>data type</u> and a <u>format</u>.

2) The <u>data type</u> is dead important, as different <u>processes</u> can be performed on different types of data. The most common data types are in the box — most programs allow others.

> TEXT e.g. Banana, NUMBERS e.g. 25.67
> DATES e.g. 26-09-82 or 26/09/82
> CURRENCY e.g. £12.59 or €4.32

3) You can set up <u>validation rules</u> for each field of your database. These can be used to check that data entered into a particular field is of the right <u>type</u> or within a certain <u>range</u>. E.g. you could set up a "Date of Birth" field to reject data if it's later than the <u>current date</u>.

Databases can be Flat-File or Relational

FLAT-FILE DATABASES

1) <u>Flat-file</u> databases are the ones that you'll be using most of the time.

2) All the data's organised into <u>one table</u>, which can be viewed by opening <u>one data file</u>.

3) Flat-file databases can be created using <u>all</u> database programs and <u>most</u> spreadsheets.

	Forename	Surname	Address 1	Address 2	Postcode	Employee Number
+	Rachel	Belgrave	5 Beanthwaite Close	Houghton	NW12 7RS	100345
+	Jenny	Underway	33 South Avenue	Beanthwaite	NW25 2HI	100346
+	Kate	Broughton	12 Bell View	Millom	LA12 7WU	100347
+	Kate	Redman	48 Rydal Gardens	Barrow-in-Oven	LA18 8GY	100348
+	Ed	Robin	28 King George Rd	Daltonia	LA29 9GG	100349
+	Dominic	Hurl	13 Devils Close	West Shields	NW13 8UV	100350

RELATIONAL DATABASES

1) <u>Relational</u> databases store the data in <u>separate</u> tables and files.

2) The tables are <u>linked together</u> by certain <u>fields</u> which they have in common.

3) E.g. the "Payroll" database table at the top of the page has the field "<u>employee number</u>" which uniquely identifies each company employee.

4) The same field is also used in this table that contains <u>employee contact details</u>.

5) Each employee number can only appear once in each table — this is called a <u>one-to-one</u> relationship.

6) You can also have <u>one-to-many</u> relationships where a piece of data can only appear once in one table but can appear many times in the table it's linked to. Phew!

This stuff could put you off relationships for life...

Relational databases take a while to get your <u>head round</u>. But you do need to know about them, so it's best to start trying to understand them <u>now</u>. Now sing after me, "Databases... what are they good for... absolutely **NOTHING**... Databases... what are they..." (Actually, they're pretty useful.)

Databases — Sorts and Queries

As well as knowing how to create a database you need to know how to <u>interrogate</u> one.
Make sure you know all the main methods explained on this page.

Database Records can be <u>Sorted...</u>

1) A <u>sort</u> is the simplest process you can do with a database. You choose a <u>field</u>, and the records are then sorted into order using the <u>entries</u> in that field.

2) Sorts can be done using <u>text fields</u> and <u>numerical fields</u>. With text fields, the entries are sorted into alphabetical order by giving all the letters a <u>numerical</u> value (e.g. A = 1, B = 2, ... Z = 26).

3) Sorts can either be in <u>ascending</u> order (with the lowest value first), or <u>descending</u> order (with the highest value first).

COMPUTERS : Table				
ID	Model	Hard Drive (Gb)	RAM (Mb)	Cost
2	GX452	60	128	£550.00
4	LEN557	20	64	£599.00
3	LEN556A	20	64	£650.00
5	JJPC3324	20	256	£655.99
6	JJPC3324DVD	30	128	£700.00
8	CAH5567RW	60	256	£729.99
7	CAH5567DVD	60	256	£729.99
1	GX3345	60	128	£799.99

This database about computers has been sorted into order of cost — cheapest first.

...Or <u>Searched</u> by Running <u>Queries</u>

1) A <u>search</u> is when the computer looks for data meeting certain <u>conditions</u>. To do this, you use a <u>query</u> — which is basically a <u>list</u> of the things you want the computer to look for.

2) <u>Simple queries</u> tell the database to look for records that meet just <u>one</u> condition.

SIMPLE QUERIES
In the database above, to do a query to find all the computers with hard drives of 60Gb, you'd put:
Hard drive = 60

=   finds values <u>equal</u> to a certain amount.

<   finds values <u>less than</u> the amount specified.

>   finds values <u>greater than</u> the amount specified.

<> finds values <u>not equal to</u> the amount specified.

<= finds values <u>less than or equal to</u> the amount specified.

>= finds values <u>greater than or equal to</u> the amount specified.

3) It's also possible to do <u>wildcard searches</u>. These are where you only know <u>part</u> of the value to search for, e.g you could search for computer models that end with 'DVD'...

WILDCARD SEARCHES...
Use * to stand for anything.
In the query
Model = "*DVD"
the asterisk can stand for anything (or nothing). So in the database above, this would give two results — JJPC3324DVD and CAH5567DVD.

COMPLEX SEARCHES...
These search for data meeting more than one condition.
E.g. in the database above, to find all the computers with 40 Gb or 60 Gb hard drives, you'd put:

Hard drive = "40" OR "60".

Or if you wanted to find computers with 60Gb hard drives which cost less than £700 you'd put:

Hard drive = "60" AND Cost < £700.

<u>Or</u> to find computers that do <u>not</u> have a RAM size of 512 Mb and whose prices is <u>not</u> more than £750, you could use:

NOT (RAM = "512") AND Cost <=£750

4) You can also do <u>complex searches</u> — these are when you use <u>AND</u>, <u>OR</u> and <u>NOT</u> to find records that meet more than one condition.

5) AND, OR and NOT are <u>Boolean Logic</u> operations. They're used in expressions which can only be either true or false.

Since CD-ROM encyclopaedias and Internet search engines work like large databases, most of the ways of searching listed here can be used on them as well.

How do I find out about myself? — search me...

This stuff's not that difficult — then again it's not the world's most exciting stuff either. It's important that you <u>try this stuff out yourself</u> — just reading about it isn't enough.

Databases — Reports

You can display the results of a query in a simple table or you can make them into a proper report...

You can make Queries into Database Reports

Reports are used to display information from a database table or query in a way that makes them easier to read and pick out the information you need.

1) When producing a report you can choose...

   – which fields you want to display

   – how you want the records to be sorted.

   – how you want the document laid out (including fonts and colours).

> Many database programs (e.g. MS Access) have wizards that will help you to create a report. They have preset layouts and styles that you can choose from.

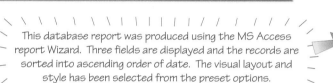

This database report was produced using the MS Access report Wizard. Three fields are displayed and the records are sorted into ascending order of date. The visual layout and style has been selected from the preset options.

Sound Equipment purchased before 2001

PURCHASE DATE	23/03/1999
DESCRIPTION	SOUND MIXER
PURCHASE COST	£300.00
PURCHASE DATE	23/03/1999
DESCRIPTION	SOUND MIXER
PURCHASE COST	£750.00
PURCHASE DATE	23/03/1999
DESCRIPTION	EFFECTS UNIT
PURCHASE COST	£500.00
PURCHASE DATE	01/02/2000
DESCRIPTION	SPEAKER
PURCHASE COST	£200.00
PURCHASE DATE	01/02/2000
DESCRIPTION	SPEAKER
PURCHASE COST	£200.00
PURCHASE DATE	01/02/2000
DESCRIPTION	STEREO AMPLIFIER
PURCHASE COST	£150.00
PURCHASE DATE	01/02/2000
DESCRIPTION	STEREO AMPLIFIER
PURCHASE COST	£130.00
PURCHASE DATE	21/02/2000
DESCRIPTION	SMALL SOUND SYSTEM
PURCHASE COST	£560.00

2) The results of a database query can also be used to create mail-merged letters. For example, an optician could send reminder letters to all people on their database who have not had an eye test for over 12 months.

3) Most database software will allow calculations to be performed on the data, and the results displayed as part of a report. For example, a publisher might use a database to store details about the weekly sales of books, with each week's sales in a separate field. The database could then add together the weekly sales for each book and display this on a report as Total Sales.

And Finally... the Good and Bad Bits of Databases

PROS OF DATABASES

1) They're a fast and efficient way of storing and accessing large volumes of data.
2) Much less storage space is required, compared to a paper based system, and data is less likely to get lost.
3) Searching for specific data is quicker and easier than using paper records.
4) It's easier to perform calculations and use the database to create other documents.

CONS OF DATABASES

1) Large databases require expensive computer hardware and software.
2) Users need to be trained in how to use them properly.

That's all I can stands. I can't stands no more....

Databases, how terribly fun. Still, they're on the syllabus, so I really had no choice but to tell you about them. Once you've got all this stuff packed in your brain, you need to sit down with your database program and start trying things out. Make a table, try some queries, create validation rules, etc. Go on, it won't bite... hard.

Section 1.2 — Revision Summary

Well done! You've just discovered the secret page at the end of Section 1.2. How very clever of you. Your intelligence will come in handy, because you've got to go through these questions and make sure you can do them all. (So perhaps finding the page wasn't that clever after all...)

1) What is the smallest part of a spreadsheet called?
   a) Sell   b) Smell   c) Cell

2) Which row is cell G14 in?

3) What is a text string?

4) How many different items of data should be entered into a single cell?

5) When creating a mail-merge data file — where should the field headings be put?
   a) In the first row   b) In the second column   c) Somewhere in Millom

6) Explain what conditional formatting is.

7) What does CSV stand for? Why is it useful?

8) What formula will Farmer Kevin put into cell B5?

9) Explain what normally happens when you copy and paste a formula into other rows or columns.

	A	B
1	Cow	Selling Price
2	Daisy	£48.50
3	Buttercup	£65.00
4	Bluebell	£70.00
5	Total Income	

10) What does "absolute cell reference" mean?

11) How would you turn "C6" into an absolute cell reference?

12) What are logic functions?

13) What does the function =IF(C2>£15,000,"No pay rise","Pay rise") mean?

14) Explain fully how a look-up table works.

15) List three essential pieces of information that should be included in spreadsheet charts.

16) Write down three different types of chart you can make with spreadsheet software.

17) What is a database?

18) What is a key field?

19) What might be the key field in a database listing information about different books?

20) What are validation rules used for in databases?

21) Explain the difference between a flat-file and a relational database.

22) What's a one-to-one relationship? What's one-to-many relationship?

23) Who will appear at the top of a list sorted in descending order of Last Name — Alice Zybrynski or Zack Alphonsus?

24) What's the difference between > and <>?

25) What's a wildcard search? How could you use one to search for all people whose last name begins McD?

26) What is Boolean logic? How can it be used to generate complex searches?

27) Look at the table and write queries to find:
   a) all the phones which cost less than £100 and have calls costing less than 20p.
   b) all the phones that aren't with O2 and have more than 100 free minutes per month.

Phone ID	Network	Price	Cost of calls (per minute)	No. of free minutes (per month)
01	O2	£59.00	£0.15	100
02	Vodafone	£132.50	£0.25	200
03	Vodafone	£85.00	£0.10	500
04	Orange	£70.00	£0.17	0
05	O2	£114.00	£0.20	100
06	Orange	£45.50	£0.30	250
07	O2	£108.99	£0.10	200
08	Vodafone	£39.99	£0.15	0

28) What are database reports? Why would you want to make a database query into a report?

29) Explain three benefits and one problem of using databases.

The Internet — Basics

The Internet — known and loved by everyone (except those who are still waiting for something to download). And as it's the biggest growth area in ICT at the moment, it's worth knowing about.

The Internet is an International Network of Computers

1) The Internet is basically a very big Wide Area Network (WAN) (see p.58).

2) The Internet was originally developed by the US Government to improve communication between its military computers. But it's since grown into what we all know today.

To Connect you need Special Hardware and Software

1) Most people access the Internet using a PC connected to a normal telephone line. Computers are attached to a telephone line via another piece of kit called a modem — this converts digital computer signals to the analogue signals carried over telephone lines (and the other way round).

2) To connect to the Internet, you use your modem to dial up a computer owned by an Internet Service Provider (ISP) — these companies have computers permanently connected to the Internet. All the information sent from your PC goes via the ISP.

3) The two most important pieces of software you need are a web browser to display web pages, and an e-mail client, which transmits and receives e-mail from a PC.

4) Web browsers sometimes need plug-ins — extra little bits of software — before they can play certain types of multimedia files, like videos for example.

The Internet has Two Main Parts

1) The World Wide Web (WWW) is the part that contains web pages. It's like an incredibly large notice board — anything posted onto the Web can be read by anyone else (although you can restrict access to sites by using user IDs and passwords).

2) Electronic Mail (E-mail) is the part where messages are sent from one person to another — it works a bit like sending a letter.

Speed of Access depends on Three Things

The speed of an Internet connection is measured in kilobits per second — KBps (i.e. how much data is transferred per second). Three things determine the speed of access:

1) **MODEM SPEED:** Most PC modems work at either 28 KBps or 56 KBps (higher numbers usually mean faster connections), but the speed of the modem at the other end also matters.

2) **THE TELEPHONE LINE:** Standard analogue lines are the slowest. But newer digital lines such as ISDN and ADSL speed up the transfer of data between the user and the ISP. Broadband is even faster and, unlike most telephone services, it's always on. You pay a fixed fee depending on just how fast your broadband link is.

> You can also measure the speed of an Internet connection using the response time — the average time it takes for a remote computer to reply.

3) **THE VOLUME OF TRAFFIC:** The more people using the Internet, the slower the speed of access. In the UK it's slower in the afternoon because that's morning in the USA — peak time for Internet use.

I searched for lobster on the Internet, but all I got was prawn sites...

Most people nowadays are pretty familiar with the Internet and e-mail — which is great, as it means this should be an easy section for you. In theory. Well, let's just read on and see...

The Internet — Navigating the Web

The WWW is <u>enormous</u> — so you need to know how to navigate your way around, which means knowing how web site addresses are structured and how to locate them.

Find Pages using Search Engines and Portals...

<u>Search engines</u> are web sites that help you search for other web sites.

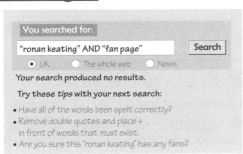

> You searched for:
> "ronan keating" AND "fan page"   [Search]
> ● UK   ○ The whole web   ○ News
> Your search produced no results.
> Try these *tips* with your next search:
> • Have all of the words been spelt correctly?
> • Remove double quotes and place +
>   in front of words that *must* exist.
> • Are you sure this "ronan keating" has any fans?

1) The basic type of search is a <u>keyword</u> search — you type in a keyword and the search engine lists a load of websites containing that keyword. Or you can do a <u>complex</u> search using more than one keyword and linking them together with <u>AND</u> and <u>OR</u>.

Most search engines work by storing details or <u>keywords</u> of different web sites, and no single search engine will have data on every web site — so it's worth using <u>more</u> than one.

2) <u>Portals</u> are web sites offering lots of different services — like search engines, e-mail, on-line shopping and so on. Originally, portals were dedicated to a particular theme (e.g. cheese, so all links were to sites about cheese) but they're usually more <u>general</u> nowadays.

...or Type in the URL

1) <u>URL</u> stands for <u>Uniform Resource Locator</u> — in other words, the address of a web page. They look a bit confusing at first — but they're easy enough once you get used to them.

2) URLs can't contain capital letters or spaces or certain types of punctuation. But some <u>full stops</u>, <u>colons</u> and <u>slashes</u> are necessary, and they have to be in <u>exactly</u> the right places... sigh.

3) Type URLs carefully — pretty obvious really — otherwise you'll either end up looking at the wrong web site, or more likely you'll get an error message. Great.

Example:	http://www.google.co.uk/advanced_search?hl=en

This is the URL of the Google "Advanced Search" web page.

<u>http</u>	This stands for <u>hypertext transfer protocol</u>, which is the language the Web uses. You don't have to type it usually, as most web browsers add it automatically.
<u>www</u>	This means that it's a web site.
<u>google</u>	This is the <u>domain name</u> — it's usually the name, nickname, initials etc. of the company, organisation, government department or whatever.
<u>.co</u>	This is the <u>domain type</u> — 'co' means the web site is run by or for a company.
<u>.uk</u>	This bit tells the computer that the web site is held on an ISP in the United Kingdom.
<u>/advanced_search?hl=en</u>	This tells the computer exactly which page within the <u>google.co.uk</u> web site you're after.

Common country codes:

us	– USA
uk	– United Kingdom
ie	– Ireland
fr	– France
de	– Germany
nz	– New Zealand

Main domain types:

com	- business (mainly USA)
co	- business (non-USA)
gov	- government
ac	- university/academic
edu	- educational institution
net	- general, often business
org	- other organisations e.g. charities

Make sure you learn domain things on this page...

See? You may have been <u>using</u> search engines and URLs since you were so high, but that doesn't mean you've actually <u>understood</u> what you're doing. It's actually kind of interesting... (just kidding).

The Internet — Navigating the Web

You can also find pages using <u>hyperlinks</u> and <u>favourites</u>/<u>bookmarks</u>. But even when you find a good page, it can take an eternity to download anything — which is where file <u>compression</u> comes in.

You can follow Hyperlinks...

<u>Hyperlinks</u> are the bits on a web page that you can click on to go somewhere else.

The pointer ⬚ changes to a <u>hand</u> ☝ <u>when you hover over a hyperlink.</u>

They're often coloured blue and underlined. They're usually displayed in a different colour (e.g. red) if you've followed them before.

1) <u>Hyperlinks</u> connect the different parts of the Web.

2) To the computer, they're an instruction to open a specified file, which is located along a particular <u>path</u> — to me, I click on a hyperlink and that's where I go next.

3) You can create them in <u>other</u> programs too, to <u>link</u> documents together, e.g. between two word processed documents on an office network, or from a spreadsheet to a web site.

...or use your Web Browser

These are standard features of web browsers to help your Internet navigation:

BOOKMARKS

Browsers can <u>save</u> URLs you use often, so you don't have to type them — a feature called '<u>bookmarks</u>' or '<u>favourites</u>'.

If you want, you can save 'bookmarks' in <u>groups</u>, which makes it easier to find the one you want — e.g. you might want to put all your favourite cheese web sites together.

BACK and FORWARD buttons

If you've followed a series of hyperlinks but want to go back to a page you saw earlier, then the browser can 'retrace its steps', and go back one page at a time. And once you've gone <u>backwards</u> like this, you can also go <u>forwards</u> again.

HISTORY

Browsers usually keep a list of all the web sites you've visited — this is called the <u>history</u>. If you want to revisit a web site, you can get the URL from the history list.

Downloading Files can take blooming Ages

1) Downloading web pages can take ages, especially if they've got lots of graphics. So the computer usually saves all web pages you view onto its <u>hard drive</u>. Then if you want to see a  page again, the computer can use the version on disk rather than reload everything down the phone line. This store of temporary web pages is called a <u>cache</u>.

2) Other files like software updates or music files can be <u>compressed</u> to reduce their size, and this means they'll take less time to download. To actually use the file once you've downloaded it, you need to have the correct software to '<u>decompress</u>' it.

Download web pages onto a laptop — cache and carry...

There's loads more about the Internet in Sections <u>3.1</u> and <u>3.3</u> of this book — about how it's used by businesses and how it affects people's daily lives. So that's a little treat for you to look forward to.

The Internet — Web Page Design

It seems like just about <u>everyone</u> has a web site nowadays — even referees.
If you want to keep up, you need to know what makes a <u>good web site</u>.

Well-Designed Web Pages follow Five Golden Rules

Web pages need to follow the same design rules as any document you want other people to read — but when you're making a web page you need to think about <u>hyperlinks</u> and <u>download time</u> as well.

1) Remember the needs of the intended audience — if possible <u>test</u> the design on the target users.

2) Keep backgrounds <u>simple</u>, and choose text formats that will contrast with it. This makes the pages easier to read on the screen, and on paper as well.

3) Keep the overall design <u>simple</u> — and use a <u>similar</u> layout on all the pages, so it's <u>easier</u> to navigate through the site.

4) Keep graphics to a <u>minimum</u> — they increase the file size and make download time longer. Loads of people don't wait more than seven seconds for a page to download — they just find another web site.

5) Keep the number of hyperlinks needed to reach anywhere to a <u>minimum</u>. Ideally, it shouldn't take someone more than four links to get to anywhere on your web site.

Web Pages are Written in HTML

1) Web pages are written in a language called <u>HTML</u> (hypertext mark-up language). Most word-processing and DTP software can convert documents into **HTML** format.

2) You can also get <u>web-design</u> programs that let you create a web page and save it as an **HTML** file.

Web Pages can contain Forms and Web-bots

As well as hyperlinks, text and images, there are two other features you need to know about.

FORMS are places where the user can <u>input</u> information. If you book a plane ticket on the Web for example, there'll be a place for you to input your destination and date of travel.

WEB-BOTS are <u>programs</u> that retrieve data from other locations on the Internet, such as search engines and <u>counters</u>.

Web-bots and cookies on the Web.

COUNTERS show how many visits (or <u>hits</u>) the web site has received. They avoid counting people twice by searching for the <u>cookie</u> that was placed on someone's computer when they first visited the site. If the web-bot finds the cookie, that person's already been counted.

COOKIES
These are just what Americans call <u>biscuits</u>. (They're also small <u>text files</u> placed onto a computer by a web page. They're mostly harmless but if you want, it's possible to stop your computer accepting them.)

Be a smart cookie — learn this page

There's a fair bit of detail on this page — so make sure you <u>know</u> it. And when you do, maybe you can go off and design your <u>own</u> web site. Even my little brother's got one now, apparently.

E-Mail

E-mail is <u>great</u>. It's good for <u>keeping in touch</u> with people who live far away, especially if you fancy them, because there are <u>no</u> embarrassing pauses while you're thinking up really witty answers.

Five Steps to Sending an E-Mail

<u>Electronic mail</u> (e-mail) is a way of sending messages (and documents) from one computer to another. The messages are often <u>text-based</u>, and are usually sent via a **PC** connected to the Internet. But you can also use a **WAP** mobile phone or a digital television.

STEP 1: <u>Create</u> the message e.g. using a word processor or the e-mail software on a computer.

STEP 2: <u>Connect</u> to the Internet.

STEP 3: <u>Press</u> the 'send' button.

...then the machines take over...

STEP 4: The message is sent from the sender's **ISP** to a '<u>mailbox</u>' in the computer system of the recipient's **ISP**.

STEP 5: The recipient later connects to the Internet, opens their e-mail account, and finds the new message — which they then download and open.

> You can also use <u>web-based e-mail</u>, which means you don't have to be connected to a particular <u>ISP</u>. You get an e-mail address by registering at a web site. Then you can e-mail from <u>any</u> on-line computer in the world — ideal if you're planning a round-the-world trip.

> For web-based e-mail, steps 1 and 2 might have to be reversed.

Take Care Opening Attachments

1) As well as text, it's also possible to send other <u>files</u> via e-mail — these are called <u>attachments</u>. For example, you could e-mail a picture or a music file to a friend.

2) Unless you're expecting to receive an attachment, treat any you receive with <u>suspicion</u> — it's easy to get a <u>virus</u> from an infected attachment.

3) It's possible to <u>view</u> an attachment without fully downloading it, or you can use virus-checking software to <u>scan</u> it before downloading. Both help to reduce the risk of getting a virus.

> The golden rule is <u>never open an attachment</u> unless you trust its source.

E-Mail has Benefits and Problems

E-mail PROS

1) It's <u>quick</u> — e-mails take seconds to send, compared to days for a letter.

2) It's <u>cheap</u> — e-mails are cheaper than posting or faxing, especially for large documents.

3) The same message can easily be sent to <u>loads</u> of different people — and if you <u>group</u> addresses, sending a message to lots of people is as easy as sending it to one person.

E-mail CONS

1) The sender and receiver <u>both</u> need Internet access and e-mail accounts.

2) The hardware and software needed is <u>expensive</u> if you just need e-mail.

3) Get a single letter of an e-mail address <u>wrong</u>, and the message won't be delivered.

4) The message will sit in the recipient's mailbox until they next look at their e-mail account.

My mate Andy's a lady's man — he gets loads of fe-mails...

People who make viruses are evil. My computer got a virus, and now I can't send any e-mails. I actually have to <u>speak</u> to my friends, and they don't think I'm witty at all any more.

Section 1.3 — Revision Summary

Well that was a nice tasty little section I reckon. But it's not over yet. Now comes the moment you've been waiting for — the test. Pit your brain and all its new knowledge against this batch of tricky questions and see if you come out tops. But watch out — there's some real tough cookies in there. Remember the way to learn — go back and repeat any questions you get wrong.

1) Explain one reason why you might need a modem to connect to the Internet.

2) Draw a diagram to show how a user connects up to a web site.

3) What are the two main parts of the Internet called?

4) What do the letters KBps stand for and what does it measure?

5) Explain three factors that affect speed of access to the Internet.

6) Explain the difference between a search engine and a portal.

7) Explain what a URL is and how it is constructed.

8) Which country has the code 'fr'?

9) Explain what a hyperlink is and what it does.

10) What is found in a history folder?

    a) a plan of the Battle of Hastings
    b) history coursework
    c) links to recently visited web sites

11) Explain how web pages that have already been visited can be displayed more quickly.

12) What's the name for the process of making a file smaller?
    What's it called when the file is expanded back to its original size?

13) Give five rules of good web site design.

14) What programming language are web pages written in?

15) What are web-bots?

16) Explain how a counter on a web site works.

17) Explain fully how an e-mail is sent and then read by the recipient.

18) What are attachments? Describe one potential problem with opening attachments.

19) Explain two benefits and two problems of using e-mail.

Organisations that Manipulate Graphics

Graphics sometimes need to be <u>manipulated</u> to make them suitable for use in a particular <u>document</u>.

Graphic Images Are Everywhere You Look

<u>Graphic images</u> are used in all sorts of documents by all sorts of organisations. Getting hold of an image to use in a document is called <u>capturing</u> the image. Once you've captured the image, you can use <u>graphics software</u> like Adobe photoshop (for photos) or Adobe Illustrator (for vector graphics) to manipulate and alter it.

There's loads more about graphic images on pages 7–9.

Below are some examples of the kind of organisations that use image manipulation and enhancement:

- Magazines, newspapers and other publishers.
- Advertising companies.
- Film and TV producers.
- The police (use a lot of image enhancement).
- Also used in brochures, catalogues, leaflets etc. produced by all kinds of companies.

Images are used a lot in the magazine industry.

Advertisers Manipulate Images Before We See Them

Whatever the type of advert, whether it's a film poster or a magazine advert for shampoo, there will have been some <u>image manipulation</u> done before it was printed.

It may come as a shock, but models and actors aren't any more <u>perfect</u> than the rest of us, and there may be some things about their appearance that need <u>correcting</u>. The organisation will take the photographs and then they can be developed and <u>captured</u> using a <u>scanner</u>. Alternatively a <u>digital</u> camera could be used. Then a variety of things could be done to the images:

spots removed · *eyelashes lengthened* · *teeth whitened* · *shine added*

- <u>Whitening</u> teeth
- <u>Removing</u> spots
- Changing eye and hair <u>colour</u>

They can even <u>distort images</u> so that people look slimmer or seem to have longer legs.
So the image you see in an advert or on a poster is probably <u>not</u> the same as the original image when taken by the camera. It's been <u>messed with</u> so that people will see it and think "Hmm, if I buy that shampoo maybe I will look just as perfect as her."

Other Organisations Enhance the Quality of Images

There are a lot of businesses these days offering to <u>restore</u> and <u>digitise</u> your old <u>photos</u>.

Photos can get <u>damaged</u> or <u>fade</u> with time. Nowadays you'd probably just print off another copy from your digital camera, but you can't do that with old photos unless they've been <u>captured</u> using a <u>scanner</u>. So some organisations offer to do that for you, and then they can use <u>image manipulation software</u> to get them looking as good as new again. For example, they can:

- <u>Cover</u> tears
- <u>Reduce</u> faded areas
- <u>Colour</u> a black and white photo

Can I borrow your airbrush, please...

Huh, the big <u>cheats</u>. I'm never buying that shampoo again. <u>Clever</u> technology though — you can alter an image <u>loads</u> and it still looks totally <u>convincing</u>. Well, except that one of Kate Winslet's legs.

Organisations that use CAD / CAM

Computer Aided Design (CAD) and Computer Aided Manufacture (CAM) are used to 'automate and control processes'. Automate means to make something work on its own. A process is just a job that needs to be done in an organisation.

CAD is Used to Design New Products

CAD involves using a computer to design a product. It can save a lot of time and effort.

1) CAD software looks similar to graphics software. It works with vector graphics and is able to take a 2D image and create a 3D model from that image automatically. Products designed using CAD can be anything from a car part to a shop front.

2) A technician using CAD will first create a feasibility drawing. This is a first draft to see if the product being designed can actually be created.

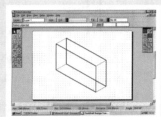

3) The software allows the technician to look at the new 3D model from all angles. It can do calculations to test how the finished product would cope with different stresses. You could use CAD to design a bridge and then test it (using the program) to make sure it can cope with different weights of traffic across it.

4) The drawings produced using CAD can be linked directly to CAM software (see below). This allows some products or parts designed using CAD to be made using CAM software and machinery very quickly and efficiently.

CAM Uses a Design to Produce a Product

1) Computer Aided Manufacture is the process of manufacturing goods using information received from a CAD package.

2) Data from CAD software is downloaded into the control unit of a manufacturing machine.

3) Components and products are then made on machines which are controlled and operated by computers rather than by a person.

4) The machines used are Computer Numerically Controlled. This means that the CAD/CAM program works out how the machine needs to move and sends this data to the machine in the form of numbers. The machine's onboard processor interprets the numbers and controls the movement of the machine.

5) Machines that are commonly controlled in this way include lathes, drilling machines and flame cutters.

CAD/CAM Systems Have Many Advantages

Using CAD/CAM can save a lot of time, effort and money, and has led to the production of higher quality and safer products.

The only real disadvantage of CAD/CAM is that it needs so much less human input than traditional systems, so there are fewer jobs available.

Of course, traditional methods worked OK sometimes.

I wouldn't mind looking at models all day for a living...

Maybe I'll be a CAD technician when I grow up. You can't fail to be impressed with all this CAD/CAM stuff. You get machines to design, test and then build everything. It's ideal for lazy people.

Organisations that Monitor Physical Data

Physical data means things like temperature, noise level and pressure. It can also include environmental data, like pollutant levels or wind speed. This data is collected using sensors.

Sensors Are Used to Monitor Physical Data

Sensors are used to take physical measurements and to convert them to computer data for analysis and interpretation. Examples of situations where sensors are used include pollution monitoring systems, traffic control systems, burglar alarms, air-conditioning systems — in fact just about anything where information from the outside world is needed. They're also used in producing all kinds of goods, from beer (where the temperature must be carefully monitored) to cars (see page 46).

Physical Data is Used to Help Control Traffic Flow

With more and more vehicles on the roads, many areas of the UK experience serious problems with congestion. To try and solve the problem, the amount of traffic on many major roads all over the UK is now monitored.

1) Electronic sensors are used to record the number of cars passing a certain point on the road.

2) The sensors are often pressure sensors which are triggered whenever a car passes over a cable which is laid across the road.

3) This information is used to identify the most congested areas, so that a solution (such as an alternative road layout or a one-way system) can be found. On motorways it's sometimes used to manage a variable speed limit system, to try and reduce the number of traffic jams.

The Met Office Uses Environmental Data to Make Forecasts

1) The Met Office are the organisation that produce weather forecasts. They collect huge amounts of meteorological data each day (see the table for examples). The data is collected with sensors at automated data-logging stations and sent to a central computer.

2) This data is then processed to produce detailed weather maps. Data collected at different times can also be combined to produce moving images of weather systems.

3) The same can be done with data collected from weather satellites — this is usually photographic images which have been converted into digital data.

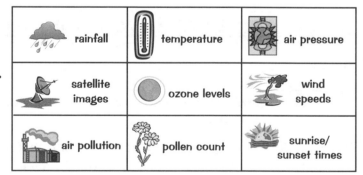

rainfall	temperature	air pressure
satellite images	ozone levels	wind speeds
air pollution	pollen count	sunrise/ sunset times

4) Collected data is fed into computer models of the way that weather patterns change and interact. This enables detailed weather forecasts to be made. As the computer models used become more sophisticated, weather predictions should become more accurate.

Guess how often the Met Office actually gets it right...

I read the other day that it's 50% of the time. Which sounds a bit rubbish to me. You might as well just guess. All that data collecting and only a 50% success rate. Flipping useless, sensors.

Developing Business Documents

You've made <u>documents</u> before — letters, birthday cards, pieces of homework etc.
And without realising it, you'll have made them fit their <u>purpose and audience</u>. Eh? Read on...

Think About <u>Who</u> a Document's For and <u>What</u> it's For

1) The <u>purpose</u> of a document means what the document is <u>meant to do</u>.
    For example, the purpose of an advert is to tell people how great a product is.

2) The <u>audience</u> of a document means <u>who</u> the document is meant for.
    For example, the audience of an advert is the people who might buy the product.

Once you know <u>who</u> you're writing for and <u>why</u>, you can think about how to <u>present</u> your document.
Some ways of writing and presenting will work better with certain <u>audiences</u> than others.

Choose the Right <u>Writing Style</u> and <u>Tone</u>

It's important to choose the right <u>writing style</u> and <u>tone</u>. Your document could be formal or
informal. It could also be friendly, persuasive, threatening, amusing etc. It's all about choosing
the <u>right words</u> to get your message across.

> For example, a <u>letter</u> inviting someone to a job interview would require a
> <u>formal</u>, serious style with no slang or made-up words. It might use long
> complicated phrases like 'Following your recent enquiry, I take this
> opportunity to advise you of our recruitment procedure... (blah blah)'.

> On the other hand, a <u>flyer</u> inviting people to a party would be
> more relaxed, chatty and <u>informal</u>. It might even try to be
> funny. Something like 'Yo, yo ho, come chill in da ghetto.'

Be Careful With <u>Layout</u> and <u>Presentation Style</u>

1) <u>Layout</u> is about <u>where</u> things are on a page and how they're
    <u>arranged</u>. For example, a <u>memo</u> will have the name of the
    person it's from somewhere near the top of the page so the
    reader sees that straight away.

2) Your <u>presentation style</u> comes from your choice of <u>colours</u>,
    <u>fonts</u> and <u>pictures</u>. For example, on an advertising poster you
    would use a <u>large</u>, <u>clear</u> font so that people could read the
    words from a distance, and <u>bright colours</u> to attract attention.

Use your style of presentation to
attract attention.

Hmmm — don't think I'll be attending THAT party...

Here's a quick recap of the important words on this page. <u>Purpose</u> means what it's for, <u>audience</u>
means who it's for, writing <u>style</u> and <u>tone</u> is about choosing the words to make it sound right,
<u>layout</u> is how the words are arranged and <u>presentation style</u> is what they look like. Phew.

Developing Business Documents

There are loads of different <u>kinds</u> of documents. Each one has certain rules or <u>conventions</u> that need to be followed to make it right for its <u>purpose</u> and <u>audience</u>.

Memos *Are Sent to People* Within the Organisation

1) These could be <u>print-outs</u>, or you can send memos by <u>e-mail</u>. Memos are used to send messages to other people <u>within an organisation</u>. You wouldn't send a memo to someone <u>outside</u> your business, like a customer.

2) A memo will have the word '<u>Memo</u>' or '<u>Memorandum</u>' at the top, plus details of who the memo's <u>for</u>, who <u>sent</u> it and the <u>date</u> it was sent.

3) The main text might have a <u>title</u>, and it'll be a fairly short message. The <u>tone</u> of the memo could be formal or informal, depending on the purpose and audience. Memos are sent for <u>lots of reasons</u>, from inviting people to a staff party to reminding staff of company rules and regulations.

Letters *Are Sent to People* Outside the Organisation

<u>Business letters</u> are always <u>formal</u>. They're structured like this:

1) The address of the <u>sender</u> goes in the top right corner of the letter. Some businesses may use their own <u>letterhead</u>, which will include their address, logo and contact details. The address of the person the letter is being sent to is on the <u>left</u>, just above the opening 'Dear Mr Smith'.

2) Letters must have the <u>correct opening</u> and <u>closing</u>:

- If you're writing to someone whose name you <u>don't know</u>, you should open your letter with '<u>Dear Sir/Madam</u>', and then you should close it with '<u>Yours faithfully</u>'.

- If you <u>do</u> know the person's name, you should start the letter with '<u>Dear Mr Jones</u>', and at the end it should be '<u>Yours sincerely</u>'.

> If you needed to send a letter quickly, you could <u>fax</u> it. A fax machine makes a copy of a printed document and sends it via <u>telephone lines</u> to another fax machine. They can also be sent using a <u>computer</u>. They're made up of a <u>fax cover sheet</u> and the document you want to send.
>
> 1) The fax cover sheet will have details of who the fax was <u>from</u>, their <u>contact details</u>, who it's <u>for</u> and the <u>subject</u> of the fax.
>
> 2) A wide variety of documents are faxed to and from organisations. These include <u>contracts</u>, <u>letters</u>, <u>CVs</u>, <u>agendas</u> and <u>minutes</u>.

Data Capture Forms *Are Used to* Gather Information

You might fill one in to open a <u>bank account</u>, or when completing a <u>questionnaire</u> or <u>survey</u>.

1) A <u>data capture form</u> should have a certain number of <u>spaces</u> to fill in information, as there will be a <u>database already created</u> to handle the information. For example, there might a line like this:

Surname

There are 20 spaces here, which means that the <u>database field</u> for Surname will be 20 characters in size.

2) Some data capture forms will have <u>limited choices</u> for the reader, such as Yes/No or age ranges.

Memo to self — learn all the fax on this page...

It's not as easy to <u>capture data</u> as it looks. You need quite a <u>big net</u>. Alright that's a <u>lie</u>, but what am I <u>supposed</u> to say about this page? I mean, for crying out loud, we all know what a <u>letter</u> is...

Developing Business Documents

The kinds of documents on this page are meant to be used <u>without</u> printing them out.
They're either worked on mainly <u>on the computer</u>, or viewed on a <u>monitor</u> or <u>multimedia projector</u>.

Web Pages Are Viewed Over the Internet

<u>Web pages</u> are mainly written in a language called <u>Hypertext Markup Language (HTML)</u>. But you can now use modern software to make web pages <u>without</u> having to understand this language.

1) Web pages are <u>multimedia documents</u>. That means they can contain loads of different kinds of information, from simple text and graphics to <u>animations</u> and <u>video clips</u> with sound.

2) Web pages are meant to be <u>interactive</u>. The reader should be able to do something with a web page, like <u>selecting</u> from a menu or clicking on a <u>hyperlink</u> to take them to another page.

3) A <u>wide audience</u> may view a web page, and it's important that you have this in mind when creating one — e.g. you might want to provide a text-only version of your page so that visually impaired people using screen-reading software can use it. But although <u>anyone</u> can view a web page, you should still design it to appeal to <u>your target audience</u>.

Interactive Presentations Use a Screen or Monitor

See pages 13 – 16 for more on presentations.

<u>Interactive presentations</u> are meant to be either <u>projected onto a screen</u> using a <u>multimedia projector</u>, or displayed on a <u>monitor</u> where people can use it to find out information.

1) Like web pages, interactive presentations are <u>multimedia documents</u>. The <u>number</u> and <u>types</u> of different media used will depend on whether the presentation will be <u>stand-alone</u> (viewed on a monitor or screen without someone talking) or part of a presentation with a <u>speaker</u>.

2) If someone is to be speaking along with the presentation, its content is likely to be <u>short bullet points</u> and <u>diagrams</u>, as the speaker will be filling in the details with his or her speech.

3) If the presentation is meant to be stand-alone (an example of this might be an interactive display in a museum), there will be more <u>detail</u> on the slides. A presentation like this will also have <u>hyperlinks</u> between slides, like on a webpage.

Your Own Documents Must Be Carefully Designed

When you're producing your <u>own</u> documents, you'll have lots of decisions to make which will be affected by the <u>purpose</u> and <u>audience</u> of your document. First you'll need to choose the right <u>document type</u>, and then think about the <u>writing style</u> and <u>tone</u>, <u>layout</u> and <u>presentation style</u>.

Here are some examples of when you might use different document types:

PURPOSE AND AUDIENCE	SUGGESTED DOCUMENT TYPE
Telling an employee they've lost their job.	Formal letter.
Inviting office staff to contribute to a leaving gift.	Informal memo.
Advertising your business's services.	Formal webpage with interactive features.
Sending a financial plan to a customer.	Fax.
Providing maps and info on local attractions at a tourist information centre.	Stand-alone interactive presentation.

Formal

Informal

Alright Bob, you're fired mate. Cheers, the Boss...

See what I mean? It's vital that your documents are <u>appropriate</u> for their purpose and audience. And once you've got the <u>document type</u> sorted, it's <u>easier</u> to decide on the tone, layout, colour, etc.

Standard Ways of Working — Safety Issues

Last couple of things you need to know about for Section 1 — health and safety, and data security. Then that's the first section all done, and you can have a little break and nurse your RSI...

Computer Use can cause Three Main Problems

There are three main problems — connected either with poor design of the equipment, or from not using the equipment properly. In each case the risk is small, but the effects can be serious.

1) Repetitive strain injury (RSI) is a general term for aches, pains and muscle or tendon damage resulting from overuse of a keyboard or mouse. Some people call it upper limb disorder (ULD).

2) Spending too long in front of a VDU can cause eye strain and headaches. The glare from the screen and poor-quality images on some old monitors can make it hard for the eyes to focus properly.

3) Circulation, fitness and back problems might result from sitting all day in front of a computer rather than walking around. This is more of a long-term health problem.

...Which have Three Main Solutions

1) Take regular breaks from computer work. Looking away from the screen, walking around and exercising your fingers and hands can also help to reduce the health risks.

AS A GENERAL RULE
1) Your forearms should be roughly horizontal.
2) Your eyes should be level with the top of the VDU.

2) Use the correct equipment. You should have:
   a) a proper computer chair with backrest,
   b) an ergonomically-designed keyboard that makes it easier to touch-type without straining fingers,
   c) good background lighting,
   d) a screen filter to reduce VDU glare.

3) Arrange the equipment properly. Adjust the chair and VDU to find the most comfortable position to work. And make sure there aren't any cables trailing around for people to trip over.

There Are Laws About Health and Safety at Work

This is covered in detail in Section 3.2, but it's worth remembering that your employer has a legal responsibility to make sure you're safe at work. He or she has to provide the equipment described above, pay for regular eye tests for employees that use computers all day, and make sure that they take regular breaks.

It's also worth remembering that employees themselves have responsibilities by law — to take sensible precautions at work and to make sure that they don't endanger themselves or others. So if you have an accident at work because you're dancing the can-can on your desk, you're not really allowed to blame the boss.

Oh, and try to come to work fully dressed...

Our model in the picture above may have great posture, but he's forgotten his clothes and could easily catch his death of cold. You see, it's the little things you have to keep an eye on, and it's all pretty common sense stuff. Regular breaks, correct equipment, remembering your trousers...

Standard Ways of Working — Security

There are three main types of network security: <u>physical</u> security, <u>access</u> security and <u>data</u> security.

Physical Security Protects the Hardware

Hardware is <u>expensive</u> — follow these 7 <u>SAD FLAB</u> rules to keep it safe.

Can you identify this?

Errmm... hang on.. Is it a toaster?

1) **Serial numbers** — Keep a record of all <u>serial numbers</u>, and mark the organisation's name and postcode on all equipment — this helps police to identify stolen property.

2) **Alarms** — Computer rooms should be protected by <u>burglar alarms</u>.

3) **Doors** should be locked when the rooms are not in use.

4) **Fire protection** — Use fireproof doors and smoke alarms. Also, automatic <u>gas-flooding</u> <u>systems</u> could be used to put out any fire to prevent water damaging the equipment.

5) **Lock** windows to prevent access.

6) **Avoid** putting computers on the ground floor of buildings, where they can be easily seen from outside.

7) **Blinds** or curtains should be closed at night, and monitors should be switched off, so the computers are less visible.

> Protect hardware with the 7 <u>SAD FLAB</u> rules.

Access Security Limits a Person's Use of the Network

1) All <u>authorised users</u> should be given <u>user names</u> and create their own <u>passwords</u>. This will limit <u>unauthorised access</u> to the network.

2) Users should <u>change</u> their password <u>frequently</u>.

3) Individual users can be assigned <u>access rights</u> — for example network managers can be given access to the software that controls how the network is run. Other users can be <u>limited</u> to <u>certain types</u> of <u>applications software</u> such as word processors.

Data Security Prevents Loss of Data

1) Some software and files can be <u>password-protected</u> so that a password is needed to <u>view and amend</u> data.

2) Files can be made <u>read-only</u>, so that they cannot be altered or deleted. Other files may be <u>hidden</u> so that they are not visible to the user.

3) Regular <u>back-ups</u> should be made of the data on the system using suitable <u>backing storage</u>. The main method used to back-up network data is the <u>ancestral method</u>.

4) <u>Back-up files</u> should be kept secure — ideally in <u>locked</u> <u>fireproof rooms</u> in a <u>different location</u> to the network.

5) <u>Archiving</u> means copying or moving a file somewhere for <u>long-term</u> storage.

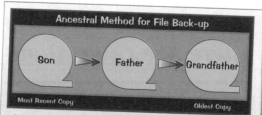

Ancestral Method for File Back-up

Son → Father → Grandfather

Most Recent Copy — Oldest Copy

The <u>son</u> is the <u>most recent copy</u> of the file. When the <u>next back-up</u> is made, this becomes the <u>father</u>.

When the <u>next back-up</u> is made the father becomes the <u>grandfather</u>. The grandfather file is deleted when a new son is created.

If the <u>original</u> file is <u>lost or damaged</u> there are <u>three back-up files</u> available.

Making three copies of everything would get my back-up...

Most of this is <u>common sense</u> — especially if you think about how a school computer network operates. It's a good idea to protect yourself from computer theft at home, too.
<u>Back-up</u> important essays or pictures onto CD, and store the CDs <u>away</u> from the computer.

Section 1.4 — Revision Summary

That's it for section 1.4. There's quite a variety of stuff covered, from graphics through business documents and on into security of data and health and safety. A real rollercoaster, without the excitement (but probably with some screaming still involved). Anyway, jot down an answer to each of these revision questions and have a glance back through the section to see if you were right.

1) Name three types of organisation that capture, manipulate and enhance graphic images.

2) Suggest three ways that an image of a model in a fashion magazine might be changed to make the model look better.

3) Suggest two things that could be done to digitally enhance the quality of some very old photos.

4) What do CAD and CAM stand for?

5) List the main features of CAD software.

6) How can CAD and CAM be used together to manufacture products?

7) Give three situations where physical data would be monitored, analysed and interpreted.

8) Explain how sensors can be used to monitor traffic and what can be done with the data collected.

9) How does the Met Office use physical data to produce weather reports and forecasts?

10) What would the purpose of a job advert be? Who would the audience be?

11) You need to write a letter inviting someone for an interview, and you also need to design the invitations to a party. Write about how the following would differ between the two documents:
   a) Tone and style.   b) Layout.   c) Use of colour, pictures and fonts.

12) If you needed to send a short message to someone in another department, what type of document could you use?

13) If you know the name of the person you're sending a letter to, what would be the correct way to end the letter?

14) What must you always include with any documents you're sending by fax?

15) On a data capture form, how many spaces would you allow for someone's date of birth?

16) Web pages are multimedia documents. What does this mean?

17) What must the reader of a web page be able to do in order for the web page to be interactive?

18) In what two ways can interactive presentations be viewed?

19) What is a stand-alone interactive presentation, and where might one be used?

20) What might a stand-alone presentation have that a presentation to be used in a speech might not?

21) What does RSI stand for, and how might it be caused by working at a computer?

22) Give three other health problems that working regularly at a computer might cause.

23) Give three ways to avoid health problems if you work regularly at a computer.

24) What are the seven rules you should follow to make sure expensive hardware is physically secure?

25) Give two ways of keeping data on networks secure.

26) What is the ancestral method for file back-up?

Meeting an Organisation's Needs with ICT

Organisations use ICT systems to meet their needs and achieve their objectives. Some of these objectives can be quite small things, but they still need effective systems to get them done.

An ICT System Has Three Main Parts

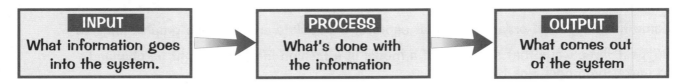

INPUT	PROCESS	OUTPUT
What information goes into the system.	What's done with the information	What comes out of the system

For example, at the supermarket checkout:

1) The input is the barcode data (entered into the scanner).

2) The process is finding the names and prices of the items in a database, and adding them up.

3) The output is the receipt with those items listed, and the total you have to pay.

Different Organisations Will Need Different Systems

Different businesses use different ICT systems depending on their particular needs.
Take the example of a video rental shop:

Video shops usually allow people to become members for free if they can provide proof of their address. They're then charged a small amount each time they hire a video.

A video shop like this has a number of needs that can be met using ICT:

- The video shop can use a database to keep a record of all its members, their membership numbers and their home addresses.

- A database would also be needed to show which videos were currently out on loan, who had borrowed them, and when they were due back.

- The shop manager can use the Internet to keep up with all the latest video releases, and could also use ICT when ordering new stock for the shop (see p.44).

- They can use spreadsheets to calculate the fines owed by members who don't return their videos on time.

- The membership database could be used with mail-merge to create marketing material telling regular members about special offers and new releases.

- It might also be helpful to keep a record of which videos are hired by which customers. This would help the video shop to tailor its marketing material to the interests of particular members, and would also help them to decide which videos are no longer popular.

Any organisation will have a list of needs that can be met by ICT like this — it just takes a bit of thinking about.

I SAY my favourite film is Kill Bill 2... (But it's really The Little Mermaid.)

Pick another organisation and think up a list of needs like the one about the video shop. You could try a restaurant, a charity shop, a hospital or a school (remember, we're not just on about for-profit organisations here). Then think of ways you could use ICT to meet the needs you identified.

ICT in the Sales Department

Organisations are divided into <u>departments</u> so that the work is easier to manage — the different departments have different <u>responsibilities</u> within the organisation. The four kinds of department you need to know about are <u>sales</u>, <u>purchasing</u>, <u>finance</u> and <u>operations</u>.

A Sales Department Uses ICT to Keep Customer Records

The <u>sales department</u> of an organisation does work that involves <u>selling</u> products or services to other businesses or people. Sales departments often use several different <u>ICT systems</u>.

1) When a new customer makes a call to a business, their details may be taken down by the sales department, and they may be given a <u>reference number</u> to use when they call next time. So, in this system:

INPUT	PROCESS	OUTPUT
Customer details	Save details to database	Reference number for the customer

2) This reference number will be used by the organisation to <u>track transactions</u>. This means that the reference number will allow the organisation to search a <u>customer database</u>, and find out if an order has been sent, for example. Or it could be used to check whether an invoice has been paid by a customer. So, in this system:

INPUT	PROCESS	OUTPUT
Reference number	Find details of order in database	Detailed information on the order

ICT Systems Can Also Be Useful in Marketing

The sales department are often involved in <u>marketing</u> the company's products and services as well, because they're regularly in <u>direct contact</u> with the customers. If a customer has bought one product or service from the organisation, then it's worth seeing if they want to buy another.

Here are a couple of ways in which businesses can <u>market effectively</u> using ICT:

1) Using a customer database to <u>mail-merge</u> (see p.6) letters and leaflets to be sent to the customer. If the organisation already has the customer's name and address saved in the customer database, it makes sense to use this information to send out <u>marketing materials</u>.

2) Sending <u>promotional e-mails</u> to customers. Often businesses will send <u>confirmation</u> e-mails when you place an order. They can then use this same address to send out marketing messages informing their current customers of new <u>special offers</u> and so on.

In order to do these two things, the business must be sure that the customer has <u>opted-in</u> to promotional mailings and e-mails. If they haven't, the organisation could be accused of sending <u>spam</u> e-mail. In each promotional e-mail there should be an <u>option</u> allowing the customer to opt-out.

But I TOLD you I hate spam!

"All our sales representatives are busy at the moment..."

...Your call is being held in a queue and will be answered shortly." That's all <u>I</u> ever seem to hear from sales departments nowadays. They keep telling me my call is <u>important</u> to them, but then refuse to answer it. It <u>hurts my feelings</u>, it really does. You've still got to <u>learn about them</u>, though.

ICT in the Purchasing Department

The purchasing department deals with goods and services that need to be bought <u>into</u> the organisation. For example, most organisations will need stationery and so on for their <u>offices</u>, and many will have to buy the materials needed to <u>make the products</u> they sell.

The Purchasing Department Handles Stock Control

Stock control is one of the purchasing department's most important responsibilities. If the business doesn't have the raw materials and other supplies it needs to function, it will start to lose money.

> For example, think about a business that makes fruit drinks. If there <u>isn't enough</u> fruit in stock, the business won't be able to make any drinks and will <u>lose income</u>. But on the other hand, if there's <u>too much</u> fruit in stock some of it will go bad before it can be used and this <u>wastes money</u>.
>
> So purchasing departments need to <u>keep track</u> of how much of everything they've got in stock. They also need to know the <u>reorder level</u> of every item — when the number of a particular item <u>falls below</u> this level, the company needs to <u>order more</u>. This will be different for every item, because it depends on how quickly the item gets used up and how long it takes to receive more.

ICT is Used to Order Goods and Keep Records

Below are some of the systems that the purchasing department might use.

1) Most stock control systems are able to respond <u>automatically</u> when new stock needs to be ordered. E.g. a <u>spreadsheet</u> or <u>database</u> might be used to keep a record of how much of each item there is in stock. As soon as this number falls below the <u>reorder level</u>, the system produces an <u>alert</u> reminding the purchasing department to order more. So in this system:

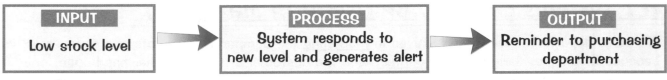

INPUT — Low stock level → PROCESS — System responds to new level and generates alert → OUTPUT — Reminder to purchasing department

Some really posh systems don't just produce an alert — they <u>send an order</u> directly to the supplier instead. So as soon as more stock is needed, it's automatically ordered. Clever.

2) Some purchasing departments use the <u>Internet</u> to buy the supplies they need. Imagine a business needs some printer cartridges. The purchasing department would access the <u>website</u> of the supplier, perhaps someone like <u>www.ebuyer.com</u> or <u>www.dabs.com</u>. They would type in their <u>account details</u> and place an order for the cartridges. They'd then receive an order confirmation from the supplier by <u>e-mail</u>. So in this system:

INPUT — Account details, and details of order → PROCESS — Record order on website → OUTPUT — Order confirmation e-mail

Stock control — more fun when the business is a farm...

...then you get to <u>chase pigs around</u> and so on, rather than just ordering stuff. The purchasing and sales departments are both <u>equally important</u> to a company — sales actually sell the stuff to make <u>money</u> for the company, but purchasing makes sure it <u>has something to sell</u>.

ICT in the Finance Department

The <u>finance department</u> keeps track of all the <u>money</u> that comes in and out of the organisation. It deals with requests for money from the <u>purchasing</u> and <u>operations</u> departments, and processes the money that comes in from the <u>sales</u> department.

Finance Departments Use Lots of Spreadsheets

Below are a few examples of <u>ICT systems</u> used by finance departments. All of them could involve <u>spreadsheets</u>. This is because spreadsheets are excellent for performing <u>calculations</u>.

Finance Departments Have to Make Sure Everyone Gets Paid

The finance department operates a <u>payroll system</u>. They could use a <u>spreadsheet</u> or <u>specialised financial software package</u> for this. The department <u>inputs</u> how much everyone gets paid by the hour, and calculates how much to pay each employee depending on how many hours they worked. The organisation also has to work out the amount of <u>tax</u> and <u>National Insurance (NI)</u> to pay using the same software. They'll then use an electronic system known as <u>BACS</u> to send the correct pay to employees' bank accounts. So, in this system:

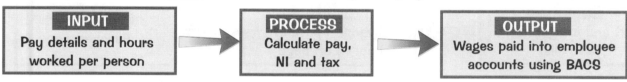

Finance Departments Have to Budget for the Year Ahead

Businesses use <u>cash flow forecasts</u> so that they don't run out of money halfway through the year. To help predict their cash flow, they use <u>financial models</u> that make use of <u>spreadsheets</u>. They take information from the year before and make predictions based on those figures. They might input <u>last year's figures</u> into the spreadsheet and make any changes necessary, e.g. they'd have to <u>adjust</u> the figures if they now had more or less staff. This kind of information could then be presented in a <u>table</u> or a <u>chart</u>, or used to help produce the yearly <u>budgets</u>. So in this system:

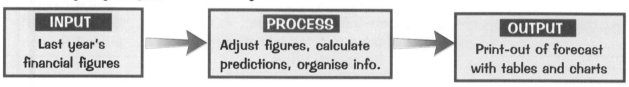

Finance Departments Have to Produce Financial Reports

At the end of each <u>financial year</u>, in April, most businesses are required by law to produce a <u>financial report</u> showing how much money has been made and spent — this is used to calculate how much tax the business owes. There are <u>specialised software packages</u> for this which have all the <u>calculations</u> already built-in. The final report is then presented as a written document. Certain parts of it might be presented as <u>charts</u> to make the information easier to interpret. So, in this system:

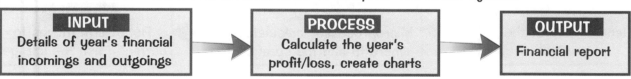

You can't take it with you, you know...

Hopefully you'll have realised by now that those little <u>input-process-output diagrams</u> are well worth learning. If you can scribble them down, they'll help <u>jog your memory</u> about the explanations that go with them. And it'll <u>save time</u> if you only have to learn a few little boxes.

ICT in the Operations Department

The operations department are responsible for the main business that the organisation deals in. If the business manufactures teapots, they're the boys that make the teapots. Simple.

Different Operations Need Different ICT Systems

The operations department is where there's the most difference between organisations. Below are some examples of systems that might be used in an operations department.

① The operations department of a newspaper is pretty big, because it's responsible for actually producing the paper. One of the jobs within it is that of sub-editor. It's the job of a sub-editor to arrange the stories written by the journalists into a form suitable for printing. So sub-editors work mainly on the layout of the pages, using special DTP software. After the sub-editor has finished their job, the finished pages are passed to the editor who can request any changes they might want. So in this system:

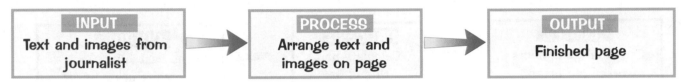

INPUT	PROCESS	OUTPUT
Text and images from journalist	Arrange text and images on page	Finished page

② The main business of a supermarket is to sell stuff. Items are placed on a checkout, and the checkout operator scans the labels with a bar code scanner. This scanner takes the bar code data, which just contains an identifying number, and finds the correct product and its price from the supermarket's database of products. Once all the products have been scanned, the operator can tell you the total cost and print a receipt. As the items are being scanned, the till computer can also adjust the price to take into account any special offers.

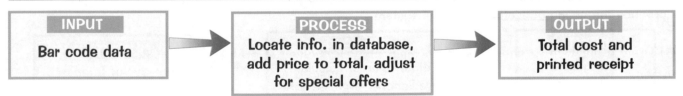

INPUT	PROCESS	OUTPUT
Bar code data	Locate info. in database, add price to total, adjust for special offers	Total cost and printed receipt

③ Many operations departments use robots. Robots can work in all kinds of environments and never get bored, tired or make mistakes — plus, you don't have to pay them. A big use of robots is in car manufacturing where they're used for a variety of tasks on the assembly line, like spray-painting the cars. The robots doing this have sensors to detect the car edges and use this information to always point the sprayer in the right direction.

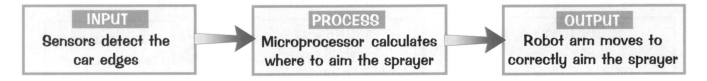

INPUT	PROCESS	OUTPUT
Sensors detect the car edges	Microprocessor calculates where to aim the sprayer	Robot arm moves to correctly aim the sprayer

What does the operations department of a hospital do?

These four departments each have their own particular job to do within the organisation, but they must also communicate well with each other, as well as with customers and suppliers. The documents businesses use to do this are covered in Section 1.4, and have a look at Unit 3 too.

Section 2.1 — Revision Summary

That's the end of section 2.1, and what a lovely short section it was too. And now I've done you some lovely questions for afters. I've got a good feeling about them, and I think you might be about to get them all first time. But if you don't, there's no need to panic — you can just look back through the section and find the answers. Phew.

1) What are the three main stages or parts of an ICT system?

2) What kind of data would a hospital need to store?

3) How could ICT be used by the hospital to meet this need?

4) Name the four main departments of an organisation.

5) What job does the sales department of an organisation do?

6) A sales department wants to use ICT to check whether an invoice has been paid by a customer. Draw a diagram to show the three main stages involved in this process.

7) Give two ways that ICT can be used to help a company with marketing.

8) Why must businesses make sure that customers can opt-out of receiving their promotional messages?

9) Explain what is meant by stock control.

10) What does 'reorder level' mean in the stock control process?

11) Explain how ICT can be used to make sure new stock is ordered in plenty of time.

12) Give another way that ICT can be used by purchasing departments.

13) What is the main job of the finance department of an organisation?

14) Why is spreadsheet software particularly useful for the finance department?

15) Describe briefly how a typical payroll system works.

16) Draw a diagram to show the three main stages involved in creating a cash flow forecast.

17) What does a financial report tell you about a business?

18) Give two ways that ICT is used by finance departments to help produce financial reports.

19) What is the main job of the operations department of an organisation?

20) Choose three types of business and explain one way that ICT is used in each of their operations departments.

Input Devices

An input device is any <u>hardware</u> which is used to <u>enter data</u> into the computer system.

QWERTY Keyboards are the Most Common Input Device

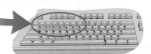

1) QWERTY keyboards are the most common type of keyboards. The name comes from the <u>first row of letters</u> on the keyboard.

2) Each key is connected to a <u>switch</u> which closes when the key is pressed. This sends a <u>signal</u> to the CPU.

3) QWERTY keyboards are based on the way typewriters were designed.

4) A problem is that keying in can be slow unless the user has been <u>trained</u> or knows how to type.

Concept Keyboards are Faster but More Limited

1) Concept keyboards are typically found in <u>shops</u> and <u>restaurants</u>. Each switch has a <u>symbol</u> (or word) on it, representing a piece of data (e.g. the <u>price</u>) stored in the computer.

2) For example, if you go to a fast-food restaurant and order a bacon-double-turnip burger, the assistant will press the picture of that burger. The CPU then tells a <u>display panel</u> to show the correct price and sends a message to the kitchen and stock-control.

Concept keyboards are <u>great</u> if you want to key in <u>similar information over and over</u> again.

Mouses and the like...

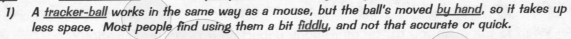

Most people find using a mouse <u>easy</u>. A mouse has <u>two main parts</u>:

1) *There are usually two or three <u>buttons</u>. When the cursor is over an icon, menu item, or the edge of a picture, the mouse buttons can be <u>clicked</u> or <u>double-clicked</u>. This gives the computer a <u>command</u>. The button can also be <u>held down</u> to <u>drag</u> something across the screen.*

2) *Under the mouse is a <u>ball</u>. The ball <u>rotates</u> when the mouse is moved across a flat surface. <u>Sensors</u> measure the movement of the ball in two directions. From this, the computer can work out the <u>direction and distance</u> the mouse has travelled. This is used to move the <u>cursor</u> on the <u>screen</u>. (N.B. optical mice use optical sensors to detect movement instead of balls).*

  <u>Laptops</u> have <u>tracker balls</u>, or little <u>pimples</u>, or touchy-feely <u>pads</u>:

  1) *A <u>tracker-ball</u> works in the same way as a mouse, but the ball's moved <u>by hand</u>, so it takes up less space. Most people find using them a bit <u>fiddly</u>, and not that accurate or quick.*

  2) *<u>Touch-sensitive pads</u> look like <u>small screens</u>. You move your <u>finger</u> across the pad to move the cursor. They use <u>less space</u> than a mouse, but they're <u>easily damaged</u> and not very reliable.*

  3) *<u>Little pimples</u> work by putting a finger on them, and pushing in a direction, which moves the cursor. They're really really small, not very accurate, and a bit weird.*

Graphics Pads make Drawing Easier and More Accurate

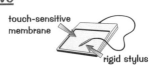

touch-sensitive membrane

rigid stylus

1) Graphics tablets are like a pen and paper. They're made of a <u>touch-sensitive</u> <u>membrane</u> (like the piece of paper) and a <u>rigid stylus</u> (like the pen).

2) The user presses on the surface with the stylus, and the membrane registers its <u>position</u>, and displays it on the <u>screen</u>.

Learn loads of facts about the mouse? — what a drag...

Nothing too tricky here. But make sure you know the <u>difference</u> between the <u>two</u> types of keyboard and the <u>three</u> types of mouse. <u>And</u> you've got to know their <u>benefits and problems</u>.

Input Devices

Four more input devices for you to get excited about. Make <u>sure</u> you know how they work.

A Joystick can Input Movement

1) These are mainly used to play <u>computer games</u> — but they can also be used to move a computer-controlled device such as a <u>robot</u> or a <u>hospital body scanner</u>.

2) The joystick is fixed to a base but can be moved in <u>any</u> direction. <u>Sensors</u> convert the movement into <u>coordinates</u>, which tell the computer how to move the <u>screen display</u> or robot device.

> Use the smart bomb.
> Use the smart bomb.

Scanners Convert Images into Digital Data

1) A scanner works a bit like a <u>fax machine</u>. A picture is passed through the scanner and is <u>converted</u> into digital data — light and dark parts of the picture are given different codes. The computer then builds up a '<u>map</u>' of the information based on these individual '<u>bits</u>' of data.

2) A problem is that these <u>bitmap files</u> can be very large and so take up a lot of <u>memory</u>. A benefit is that the scanned image can be <u>manipulated</u> and <u>edited</u> easily and quickly.

3) Small scanners are usually <u>hand-held</u>. Larger <u>flat-bed</u> scanners fit onto a worktop.

OCR Scanners can Read Text

1) OCR stands for <u>Optical Character Recognition</u>. OCR software takes the scanned digital information and looks for familiar <u>patterns</u> that might make up <u>letters or numbers</u>.

2) The scanned text can be <u>edited</u> using word-processing software.

3) This makes it quick and easy to enter <u>large blocks of text</u>. But the software is not <u>perfect</u>, so the result needs to be <u>proof-read</u>. Also, most OCR software <u>cannot cope</u> with text in <u>columns</u>.

Don't forget MICR for Cheques and OMR for Registers

MICR — Magnetic Ink Character Recognition	OMR — Optical Mark Recognition
MICR is used by <u>banks</u> to process the payment of <u>cheques</u>. At the bottom of cheques are numbers printed with ink containing <u>iron</u>. When the ink is <u>magnetised</u> a scanner can read the numbers and so know which account to take the money from. This is very fast and <u>almost 100% accurate</u>. But the system is <u>very expensive</u>.	OMR is used in some schools to take the daily class register. The teacher fills in different <u>boxes</u> with a pencil if a pupil is present or absent. A scanner detects the <u>carbon</u> in the boxes on the page and <u>inputs</u> the data into the computer system. The system is <u>quick and accurate</u> — but <u>only</u> if the OMR sheet is filled in <u>properly</u>.

Credit Cards have a Magnetic Stripe on the Back

(Unsurprisingly called <u>Magnetic Stripe Cards</u>.)

magnetic stripe

1) Magnetic stripe cards are made by sealing a short length of <u>magnetic tape</u> into the surface of a plastic card.

2) They <u>carry information</u> so the computer can identify the customer (credit/debit cards) or the number of units available (phone cards).

3) Newer cards use a <u>microchip</u> to store the information instead.

Don't scan this page — read it slowly...

There are loads of different kinds of <u>input devices</u> (just look at the next page, for example) but I reckon the most important are the <u>keyboard</u>, <u>mouse</u>, <u>scanner</u>, <u>bar code readers</u> and <u>scanners</u>. You need to be able to identify them, and know the purpose and characteristics of each.

Input Devices

The last page of input devices. Look — it's the only rainbow page in the book. You've got to read it.

There are Seven More Input Devices

1 **DIGITAL CAMERAS** are a bit like scanners. They save an image as a series of dots called pixels. The image can then be uploaded to a computer and edited using photo-editing software.
Benefits — photographic film is not needed and the image is available for immediate use.
It can also be sent via an e-mail attachment to anywhere in the world.
Problems — high-resolution images use lots of memory and currently use a lot of battery power.

2 **LIGHT PENS or LASER SCANNERS** are used in supermarkets and libraries. They are used to read a bar code which contains data about the product being scanned.
Benefits — it makes buying goods faster and reduces the chance of human error.
Problems — the system is expensive and depends upon the data in the bar code and the computer system being accurate.

3 **VIDEO DIGITISERS** convert analogue video pictures from a videotape or video camera into digital images which can then be manipulated using imaging software. This is called image grabbing.
The technique is used to make special effects in music videos and cinema movies.
Benefit — effects can be made that are impossible in real life.
Problem — the cost.

4 **TOUCH-SENSITIVE SCREENS** are a bit like concept keyboards — but instead of pressing a key, you touch the picture or word on the screen. Most use a grid of infra-red beams over the screen to sense where your finger is. *(Some use a see-through membrane instead of infra-red beams.)*
They're used a lot in information centres and quiz machines in pubs.
Benefits — easy to use and you can have different options each time the screen display changes.
Problems — more expensive than a keyboard, and inaccurate if you've got really fat fingers.

5 **MICROPHONES** are becoming increasingly used as an input device.
They are used to input data into voice-recognition systems, which convert sound into text or commands for the computer. They are also used to record sound so it can be stored digitally and sent over the Internet or e-mail.
Benefit — you can use dictation instead of having to type.
Problem — the data uses a lot of memory.

Yes, that's a microphone.

6 **SENSORS** are hardware that record environmental information and convert it into data.
For example, fishing fleets use sensors to monitor weather conditions — accurate weather data is vital for safety reasons. Other examples of sensors include temperature sensors, light sensors and infra-red sensors (which are used in burglar alarm systems).

7 **TOUCH-TONE TELEPHONES** have a different tone for each button on the keypad. This sound is transmitted over the phone line and can be used to input commands into the system at the other end of the line. They are used by cinemas to run on-line box offices, by banks to do direct banking, and by a whole load of other businesses in their telephone helplines.

Image-Grabbing — don't do it in your local art gallery...

Phew, that's a load of input devices to remember. And you've got to know all their details.
You could make a table with headings for device, how it works, benefits and problems to help you remember them all. Fun, eh.

The CPU

The Central Processing Unit is the <u>brains</u> of a computer system, where all the input data is processed. You need to know the <u>three main parts</u> of the CPU — and what happens in each one.

The Control Unit makes the System Work

The Control Unit (CU) <u>coordinates</u> the work of the whole computer system. It has <u>three main jobs</u>:

1) It controls the <u>hardware</u> attached to the system. The CU <u>monitors</u> the hardware to make sure that the <u>commands</u> given to it by the current program are <u>activated</u>.

2) It controls the <u>input</u> and <u>output</u> of <u>data</u>, so all the signals go to the right place at the right time.

3) It controls the <u>flow of data</u> within the <u>CPU</u>.

The ALU is where Data Processing Happens

ALU stands for <u>Arithmetic and Logic Unit</u>. It's where the computer <u>processes</u> data by either <u>manipulating</u> it or <u>acting</u> upon it. It has <u>two parts</u>:

1) <u>Arithmetic part</u> — does exactly what it says on the tin: it does <u>calculations</u>.
E.g. a greengrocer's till working out that if 1 kg of turnips costs 30p then 2 kg costs 60p.

2) <u>Logic part</u> — makes decisions, like whether a number is bigger than –5.
E.g. the greengrocer's computer will switch the freezer's cooling unit on if the temperature of frozen turnips recorded by a temperature sensor rises above –5 °C.

The IAS is where Active Data is Stored

1) The <u>Immediate Access Store</u> (<u>IAS</u>) holds any data and programs needed by the computer when they're being used. The CPU reads data and programs kept on the <u>backing storage</u> and stores them <u>temporarily</u> in the IAS's <u>memory</u>.

2) It normally takes <u>longer</u> to read from the backing storage than from the IAS. So the IAS makes the <u>access time</u> much <u>shorter</u>.

3) <u>Backing storage and memory</u> are covered on p56/57.

A big Diagram of the CPU to Remember

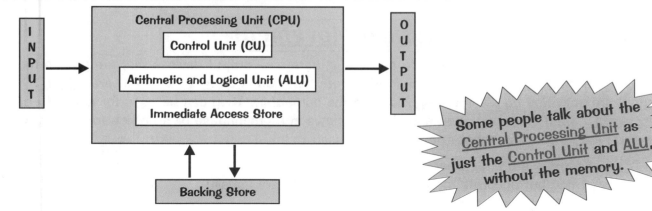

Some people talk about the <u>Central Processing Unit</u> as just the <u>Control Unit</u> and <u>ALU</u>, without the memory.

Well kids, what's YOUR favourite unit in the CPU...

The CPU is <u>pretty technical</u> stuff. And fairly mind-numbing. Luckily you only have to know a little bit about it — everything that's on this page basically. Once you've read this page, you'll be able to explain what happens in <u>each part</u> of the CPU. Sounds like a bundle of laughs.

Output Devices

An <u>output device</u> is any hardware used to <u>communicate the result</u> of data processing carried out by the CPU. You need to know <u>how</u> each one works and <u>when</u> it should be used.

VDUs give a Visual Display

A <u>Visual Display Unit</u> (VDU) or <u>monitor</u> is the most common output device. They're used when visual information is needed but a permanent record isn't. Monitors <u>differ</u> from each other in:

1) <u>Size</u> — measured in inches across the <u>diagonal</u>. A typical general PC monitor has a size of around <u>17 inches</u>. Laptops have a screen about 12 inches across.

2) <u>Resolution</u> — measured by the number of <u>pixels</u> or <u>dots</u> that make up the image viewed on the screen. The main sizes are high (1024×768 pixels), medium (800×600) and low (640×480). The resolution on most laptops is 800×600.

Graphics designers and desktop publishers who want to see a whole design or page in great <u>detail</u> should use a <u>large, high-resolution monitor</u>.

The <u>two main types</u> of monitor are:

1) <u>Cathode Ray Tubes</u> on PCs. CRTs are the same as the ones in TVs. They can <u>damage</u> the <u>eyes</u> if used for long periods so users need to take precautions (see page 39 on health and safety).

2) <u>LCDs</u> — this stands for <u>liquid crystal display</u>, and these monitors have a <u>flat screen</u>. They're used in laptops, and they're becoming more popular for desktop PCs too. They have a number of <u>advantages</u> over CRTs — they're lighter and take up less space, they use less power, emit less heat and don't flicker. But they're also <u>more expensive</u>.

Sound can be Real or Synthesised

1) Since sound can be recorded <u>digitally</u> and stored as <u>data</u>, it can also be <u>processed</u> and <u>output</u> through a <u>speaker</u>. This is how most <u>digital sampling</u> on modern music happens.

2) It is also possible to convert <u>characters</u> into <u>sound</u> through a <u>voice synthesizer</u> — this is called <u>speech synthesis</u>.
It is used by people who are <u>visually impaired</u>.
It is also used to give out telephone numbers on directory enquiries and confirm customer details on automated telephone payment systems.

> The <u>problem</u> with voice synthesizers at the moment is that they don't sound very <u>human</u>. This is because each word is usually pronounced in the same way regardless of the <u>context</u> of the <u>sentence</u>. But, they're slowly getting better...

Actuators Control Physical Movement

A <u>control interface</u> can also be used to operate <u>actuators</u> — output devices that are able to move and perform mechanical tasks. The main actuators that you need to know about are <u>motors</u>. <u>Motors</u> are activated by electrical signals from the computer. They can be used for a variety of things, e.g. to automatically open and close windows in a greenhouse or an office to regulate the temperature, or to move robot arms in a factory.

a) <u>Stepper-motors</u> are ones where the signal moves the motor in a series of tiny but accurate steps. Flat-bed scanners are usually powered by stepper-motors.

> When are they going to invent a stepper motor?

b) <u>Servo-motors</u> are ones where the signal enables the motor to move continuously at high speed. They're used to power computer-operated drills.

I told my girlfriend I had a new VDU — she went mad...

Talking computers. See — you'd have missed out on that if you'd done Textiles...

Output Devices

Printers are used to produce a permanent hard copy of the information on paper. There are three main types of printer. You need to learn how they're different and their advantages and disadvantages.

Dot-Matrix Printers are Cheap but Not Very Cheerful

They're the cheapest type of printer to buy and operate. They have two main parts:

1) The printhead is a matrix of pins — either 9 or 24 pins, arranged in a vertical line or a block. Each character is formed by using a set pattern of some of the pins.

2) The ribbon is a strip of material with ink on one side. The printhead pins push the ribbon onto the printer paper to print dots. At normal reading distance the dots seem to form characters.

ADVANTAGES OF DOT-MATRIX PRINTERS	DISADVANTAGES
Cheap, with low operating costs. Can print on continuous stationery or multi-part stationery.	Low resolution, very slow and noisy.

Laser Printers are Ace but Expensive

Laser printers are called page printers because the data to be printed is sent to the printer in complete pages — a page at a time. They work in a very similar way to photocopiers and have four main parts:

1) Electrostatic rotating drum — has an electrical charge.

2) Laser — etches onto the drum a negative image of the page to be printed. Where the laser hits the drum the electrical charge is removed.

3) Toner cartridge — contains ink. When the drum passes over the toner cartridge the ink is attracted onto the charged areas of the drum. The ink is then transferred onto the printer paper.

4) Fuser unit — heats the paper to fuse the ink onto it.

ADVANTAGES OF LASER PRINTERS	DISADVANTAGES
Very high resolution, very fast and very quiet.	Expensive (but getting cheaper) and expensive to repair. Can't use continuous or multi-part stationery.

Ink-Jet Printers are a Good Compromise

1) These cost less than laser printers and produce better quality printouts than dot-matrix printers.

2) The main component is the printhead. This has lots of tiny nozzles or spouts through which small jets of ink are sprayed onto the paper.

3) In some printers the nozzles are controlled by crystals inside the printhead, which change shape when an electrical current is passed through them. In others, the ink is heated so that it expands and pushes through the nozzles onto the paper. Continuous flow printers squirt ink continuously from the nozzles, then the unused ink is electrically charged and diverted back by charged plates.

4) There are lots more nozzles on an ink-jet than dots on a dot-matrix — so the resolution's better.

5) A bubble-jet printer is an ink-jet printer that works by heating the ink.

ADVANTAGES OF INK-JET PRINTERS	DISADVANTAGES
Good resolution, cheap and small.	Slow(ish) and expensive to run.

Buy our printers — they're ace, but they cost a fortune...

If you think this is dull, just wait till you get to the pages on data storage...

Ports and Cables

Ports and cables sound quite complicated when you don't know what they are.
But believe me, they're actually very simple. Dull, but very simple.

Ports and Cables are Just Used to Connect Devices

Ports and cables are used to connect peripherals (which means input, output and storage devices) to the CPU. Which is a pretty important job, when you think about it.

1) **CABLES** — Cables are, well, cables. They might be metal wires or fibre-optic cables. They connect the hardware devices, like keyboards, scanners, monitors and the rest to a computer. They're often also used to connect the terminals in a network.

2) **PORTS** — Nothing at all to do with shipping. If you follow the cable from your monitor or mouse, it'll lead to a place where it joins the back of the main bit of your computer. That's a port. It's just a point on a computer where you can connect peripherals.

There are Three main types of Port

1) Parallel port — Often used to connect printers. They allow data to be transmitted down parallel wires simultaneously. This makes them fast, but the signals can be distorted if they have to travel down a long cable.

2) Serial ports — Often used to connect communications devices such as modems. They transfer data in a single stream along a single wire. This makes them slower than parallel ports, but they're also cheaper, need less cable, and signals are not distorted through longer cables.

3) Universal serial bus (USB) ports — These are a newer type of port, and are expected to eventually replace serial and parallel ports to connect most peripherals. Most desktop PCs now have one or two USB ports. They work in a similar way to a telephone line, and have several advantages over serial and parallel ports:

   • They can transmit large volumes of data very quickly (much quicker than parallel ports can).
   • They can communicate with up to 127 USB peripherals at once.
   • Low-power devices (e.g. modems) connected via a USB port can run from the computer without needing their own power supply.

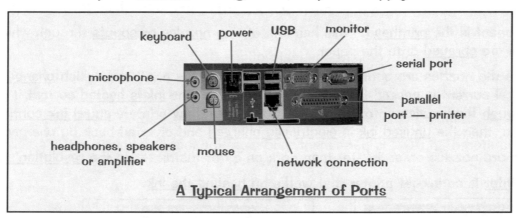

A Typical Arrangement of Ports

Universal serial bus — transporting cornflakes for all...

Don't worry too much about this page. It's pretty obvious what cables are, and ports are just the connections between your computer and all the stuff you attach to it. In fact, the only real problem with this page is the joke at the top of this tip, and we're hoping for an improvement by the next one.

Data Storage — ROM and RAM

You should remember that the Immediate-Access Store (IAS) is where the CPU holds the data that it's processing — it's the computer's memory, if you like. You need to know about the two types of memory — and why it's important to save your computer work regularly.

RAM is Temporary Memory

1) RAM is short for Random-Access Memory.

2) RAM stores data as temporary electrical signals. If the electrical power's switched off — for example, during a power cut or when a laptop battery fails — then all of the data that was stored in RAM is lost.

3) That's why it's vital to save your work regularly. Helpfully, a lot of modern software will either save your work automatically every few minutes, or give you a prompt to remind you to save it yourself. The timings for these features can usually be set by the user.

It's the shepherd's next move. Fear is in his heart. He knows that ram's volatile.

4) Because it is never stored permanently, and can easily be lost, RAM is also known as volatile memory.

5) The amount of RAM a computer has will influence its processing power, speed, and how many programs it can run at the same time. For example, a computer with 256 megabytes (Mb) of RAM will be able to run complex programs more quickly than a similar computer with only 128 Mb of RAM.

6) Lots of people confuse RAM and backing storage on the hard drive — but they're different. The computer stores programs and data that it needs quickly in RAM (if there's room), because it's much quicker to access. But information in RAM needs to be saved on the hard drive before you switch the computer off, otherwise it'll be lost.

ROM is Permanent Memory

1) ROM is short for Read-Only Memory.

2) Data and programs essential for the CPU to start working are put onto the ROM by the manufacturer of the computer system. But no new data or programs can be written to the ROM by the user.

What did you say ROM was? / ROM is permanent memory / Uh-huh, so what is ROM then? / I said, "ROM is permanent memory."

3) ROM is permanent memory, and contains the instructions that enable the operating system to be loaded into the IAS (i.e. the computer's memory) from the backing store (i.e. hard drives etc.). (However, sometimes the computer operating system is stored on ROM.)

4) The amount of ROM in most computers is small compared with the amount of RAM.

5) Because the data stored on ROM is permanent, and won't be lost in a power cut, it's called non-volatile memory.

6) Lots of people also confuse ROM with backing storage on the hard disk — don't be one of them. Luckily backing storage is covered on the next page, and that'll be an end to all this confusion.

RAM — force it into your head...

I reckon this is a fairly straightforward page. (Hmm....) Make sure you get your head round the difference between ROM and RAM, then you've basically done the hard bit. But there's still one other potential trap that you have to avoid — not confusing either of these with the hard drive.

Data Storage — Backing Storage

A <u>backing store</u> (also known as <u>secondary storage</u>) is any data-storage area outside the CPU. You need to know <u>what</u> the main storage areas are, <u>how</u> they work, and <u>what</u> their main uses are.

Hard Disks are the main Internal Backing Store

1) <u>Hard disks</u> are usually found inside computers. They're <u>rigid</u> circular plates that have been <u>magnetised</u>, and each <u>hard drive</u> usually contains several disks stacked on top of each other.

2) Each disk contains lots of <u>concentric tracks</u>, and these tracks are divided into <u>sectors</u>. The data is stored in the sectors. Most disks can store data on <u>both sides</u>.

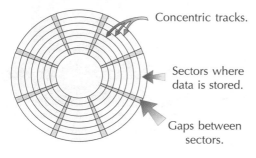

Concentric tracks.

Sectors where data is stored.

Gaps between sectors.

3) The disk <u>rotates</u> at between 5400 and 7200 revolutions per minute (rpm) and <u>read/write heads</u> (one on each side) float just above the surface of the disk. They're so close that a speck of dust would ruin the hard drive — so the disk drive is kept in a <u>sealed unit</u>.

4) It's possible to connect an <u>external</u> hard drive if additional storage is needed.

5) The main benefit of hard drives is that they have a pretty <u>large capacity</u> — <u>20 gigabytes</u> or more (1 gigabyte = 1024 megabytes) is now common in a desktop, and <u>8 gigabytes</u> in a laptop.

6) One problem is that the hard drive is housed <u>inside</u> the computer, so it's not easy to use it on a different machine (although you can buy special removable hard drives). Also, if there's a problem with the hard drive, all of the data stored on it may be lost.

Floppy Disks are a Common External Backing Store

1) The most common external backing store is a <u>3.5-inch floppy disk</u>.

2) A floppy disk is a circular piece of <u>magnetised plastic</u>, but being floppy it's easily damaged — this is why they have a protective <u>hard plastic</u> sleeve.

3) They work in a pretty similar way to hard disks. The main difference is that the read/write heads <u>access</u> the disk through holes in the protective sleeve.

4) They have a small <u>tab</u> which can be slid down to make the disk <u>read-only</u>. This helps to reduce the chances of data being accidentally <u>overwritten</u> and lost.

5) Floppy disks are small and portable, so you can easily transfer data between different computers. Unfortunately, the amount of data a floppy disk can hold is limited — normally only <u>1.44 megabytes</u>. Accessing data can sometimes be very <u>slow</u> too.

6) Also, the <u>read/write head</u> actually makes contact with the disk, which reduces its <u>lifespan</u> and increases the chances of <u>data corruption</u>. The solution is to make <u>back-up copies</u> of floppy disks.

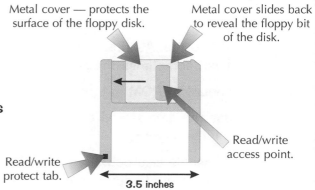

Metal cover — protects the surface of the floppy disk.

Metal cover slides back to reveal the floppy bit of the disk.

Read/write access point.

Read/write protect tab.

3.5 inches

Back-up — the type of putting you apply to fallen things...

Hard and floppy disks are similar in some ways, but are used for different reasons. Hard drives are much <u>quicker</u>, and can hold far more data, so they're used for most things. But floppy disks can be safely stored away from the computer, and so are useful for <u>backing up</u> important files.

Data Storage — Backing Storage

Wonderful news — there are some more types of backing storage for you to enjoy.
Once again, make sure you know <u>how</u> each one works and <u>what</u> its uses are.

Magnetic Tape can Back-up Large Amounts of Data

1) <u>Magnetic tape</u> is often used when large amounts of data need to be backed up.
   The data is written to and read from the tape in the same way as in a <u>video recorder</u>.

2) With magnetic tape, large amounts of data can be stored relatively <u>cheaply</u>.
   This makes them ideal for backing-up a whole <u>hard drive</u>.

3) However, <u>access time</u> is <u>slow</u>, because the <u>read/write head</u> can't go straight to a particular
   bit of data — it has to wind through the whole tape. This is called <u>serial</u> or <u>sequential access</u>.

Optical Disks have Fast Access Times

<u>Optical disks</u> include compact discs (CDs) and DVDs. They store digital data as <u>pits</u> (i.e. little
indentations) on the surface of a <u>reflective disc</u>. A <u>laser beam</u> is moved across the surface of the
disk — and the length of the reflected beam is used to <u>read</u> the data.

There are four main types of optical disk:

1) **CD-ROMs** are the oldest type. They can only be used to <u>read</u> data, but they hold loads more
   than a floppy disk can — around <u>650 megabytes</u>. Software is usually sold on CD-ROM.

2) **CD-Rs** are sold as <u>blank CDs</u>, but can have data <u>written</u> onto them only <u>once</u> (and you need
   a special kind of CD drive to do it). After that they work in the same way as CD-ROMs.
   Both CD-ROMs and CD-Rs are known as <u>WORM</u> disks — "Write Once and Read Many times".

3) **CD-RWs** are becoming increasingly popular. RW stands for <u>Read and Write</u>.
   They're like a CD-R that can have old data <u>deleted</u> and new data <u>written</u> onto the disk.

4) **DVD** stands for <u>Digital Versatile Disk</u> (or <u>Digital Video Disk</u>). They're like CDs but hold much
   more data — up to <u>17 gigabytes</u>. As a result they can store whole films digitally. <u>DVD-RAM</u>
   systems (basically DVDs that can be used to write data to) are gradually replacing home video.

A big 'plus' with any kind of optical disk is that <u>direct access</u> to the data is possible — the laser can
travel directly to where the data is stored. This means <u>faster access times</u> than with magnetic tape.

ZIP Disks are like Gigantic Floppy Disks

<u>ZIP disks</u> are larger and thicker than normal floppy disks — but work in pretty much the same way.
They need their own special <u>ZIP drive</u>, but the disks can hold
<u>100</u>, <u>250</u> or even <u>750 megabytes</u> of data — far more than
a floppy. They're good for backing up important files.
However, if CD-RW and writable DVD carry on getting more
popular, they might become <u>obsolete</u>.

DATA STORES ARE FRAGILE
And one last thing you should know
about data stores — they're like
<u>delicate flowers</u>, so protect them
from heat, cold, water, magnetic
fields, meteor showers...

CD, DVD, CD-R, CD-ROM, CD-Zzz zzzz zzz zz ... ...

All good things must come to an end — including two pages of <u>backing storage devices</u>. Don't
forget, by now you should know the <u>name</u> of each type of backing storage, its <u>purpose</u> and its
<u>characteristics</u> (including advantages and disadvantages). If you don't, read the pages again. No,seriously.

Networked Systems

Networks are always being mentioned in ICT, and everyone nods and smiles and doesn't really think much about what they actually are. Well, this is where you get to find out. It's thrilling, isn't it.

A Network is Basically a Group of Computers

A computer network is a group of two or more computers that are connected together so they can share and exchange data. There are two main types:

1) Local area network (LAN) — Confined to a small area, usually one building. The computers are connected directly using cables. Most organisations with more than two or three computers will have them connected in a LAN. This lets each individual workstation access the main file server (where all the data is stored), and this main file server can automatically back up stored data at regular intervals so that nothing gets lost.

2) Wide area network (WAN) — Can connect computers anywhere in the world. WANs need long distance communication technologies, e.g. telephone networks, satellite links, radio waves. The Internet's the best-known example of a WAN. It allows information to be shared worldwide.

A Network uses Special Hardware

1) File Server — This is the computer in a network that controls the flow of data through the network. It sometimes also stores the programmes and files that are used by the network.

2) Network Interface Card (NIC) — This is needed to connect computers in a LAN. Each computer in the network must be fitted with an NIC, and then the cables that connect them plug into the NIC.

3) Modem — This is needed to connect to a WAN like the Internet. It lets computers transfer data along a telephone cable. A modem does this by converting the digital output of a computer into analogue signals, which can travel down a telephone line. This is then converted back into digital by another modem at the other end of the line.

4) ISDN — Stands for integrated services digital network. It uses the telephone lines like a modem, but it's faster because all the connections communicate digitally using a special private line. It's expensive, so tends to be used mainly by businesses.

5) ADSL — Stands for asymmetric digital subscriber line. It's a type of broadband, and it allows more information from the site you're accessing to reach your computer, at the expense of the information travelling in the opposite direction. It still uses an ordinary phone line, and is at least 40 times faster than an ordinary modem.

Network Protocols are a Sets of Standards

Different computers from different suppliers aren't really designed to communicate with each other. Things like speed of data transfer, data format and the language used by the operating system will be different. Network protocols have been agreed so there are sets of standards about this stuff. This lets computers that use the same protocol link together and exchange data.

Networking — it can really help you feel more connected...

Most people don't even think about how networks join computers together across the world. Learn all about it and amaze your friends and family with your geeky knowledge.

Section 2.2 — Revision Summary

Section 2.2 is pretty important I reckon. It gives you all the information you need on the bits and bobs that make up a computer system. And now you've learnt all the stuff, it's time to test yourself with some fiendishly tricky questions — so you can see how much of this stuff you've really understood.

1)   Describe how a mouse works.

2)   Explain one difference between a touch-sensitive pad and a mouse.

3)   What type of file is created when an image is put through a scanner? Why is it called this?

4)   What do the letters OCR, MICR and OMR stand for? How are they different?

5)   List five other input devices — and explain how they work.

6)   Dozy Doris has been asked to perform the following tasks. For each one list the input device that she should use:
      a) type text to create a letter,
      b) record a sound message to appear on a web site,
      c) take a photo of herself to e-mail to a friend.

7)   What are the three parts of the CPU called? What does each one do?

8)   A business needs to produce a glossy and attractive brochure to advertise their products. Suggest which type of printer they might use and explain your answer.

9)   The same business needs to print out a lot of copies of invoices. These will not be seen by customers, only by staff. Give one reason in favour of using a dot matrix printer to print the invoices, and one reason against.

10)   The invoices will be printed in a busy office where staff will be taking phone orders from customers. How might this help them decide whether or not to use a dot matrix printer?

11)   How does a laser printer work? Give two advantages and one disadvantage of laser printers compared to dot-matrix printers.

12)   What is meant by the term peripherals?

13)   Explain the difference between parallel ports and serial ports.

14)   Give three advantages of USB ports over the other two types of port.

15)   What is the difference between ROM and RAM?

16)   Explain four differences between hard and floppy disks.

17)   What does WORM mean? Give the name of two types of WORM disks.

18)   I want to store a recording of a film that's half an hour long. I could use a CD, a DVD or a videotape. Explain the advantages and disadvantages of each.

19)   What is a network? Name the two main types of network.

20)   How does a modem work?

21)   What does ASDL stand for? What advantage does it have over a modem?

22)   Explain what a network protocol is.

Identifying the User Requirements

Systems analysis is the way that existing information systems are turned into new improved ones. One of your big coursework tasks is to become a systems analyst and solve a problem using ICT. This section will provide you with a nice foundation for doing it.

The System Life Cycle Shows All the Stages

This diagram called the system life cycle summarises what a systems analyst does.

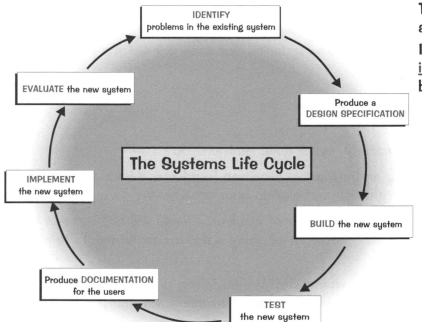

The Systems Life Cycle

- IDENTIFY problems in the existing system
- Produce a DESIGN SPECIFICATION
- BUILD the new system
- TEST the new system
- Produce DOCUMENTATION for the users
- IMPLEMENT the new system
- EVALUATE the new system

This diagram should help you to see how all the bits in this section fit together.

It also shows the systems analyst's job isn't finished when the new system has been implemented.

I'm a cisterns analyst.

The First Step is to Find Out What the Problem is

1) There are often two main problems with existing systems.
   Firstly, there might be problems with a manual system where introducing a computerised system would make things better. Secondly, there might be problems because the existing computer system is unable to cope with the information processing demanded of it.

I just can't cope with the information processing demanded of me.

2) In order to identify the problems the systems analyst needs to interview users of the system to find out their experiences; analyse the results of questionnaires given to the users; observe people using the system; study documents such as user guides, printouts and error reports.

3) From this research the systems analyst should understand how the present system works and what the problems are.

4) This information is then used to help analyse the new system and produce the feasibility study.

Identify the problem — GCSEs, they're the problem...

That circle diagram thing up there provides a really good summary of the systems analyst's job. And since you'll be becoming a systems analyst for your coursework, it also provides a handy overview of the things you're going to need to do.

Identifying The User Requirements

The next stage for the systems analyst is to think about the requirements of the new system and how much of difference it could make — this is called a <u>feasibility study</u>.

Decide on the <u>Objectives for the New System</u>

My objective is to increase the number of evenings I spend at the movies each week with Alice Trubshaw of the Accounts department from zero to one.

1) <u>Objectives</u> are specific <u>outcomes</u> that can be used to <u>test</u> whether the new system is an <u>improvement</u> on the existing one. They are also called <u>performance criteria</u> and <u>evaluation criteria</u>.

2) An <u>example</u> would be, "to <u>reduce</u> the <u>time</u> needed to <u>process</u> the data by <u>25%</u>". This is a <u>good</u> objective because it can be tested by <u>measuring</u> and then <u>comparing</u> the time taken on the old and new systems.

3) There should be several objectives for a new system.

Identify the <u>Hardware and Software</u> <u>Needed</u>

1) In order to identify the hardware and software needed the systems analyst needs to <u>have an idea</u> of <u>how they think</u> the new system <u>might work</u>.

2) The hardware and software should be chosen by <u>comparing it with alternatives</u>. A good example is the decision about whether to use a laser, ink-jet or dot-matrix <u>printer</u>.

3) The decisions made here may be <u>changed</u> once the analyst moves on to the <u>design stage</u> of the system life cycle. But without some <u>guesses</u> at this stage they won't be able to <u>estimate</u> the likely money <u>cost</u> of the new system.

Carry out a <u>Cost-Benefit Study</u>

1) <u>Cost-benefit analysis</u> answers the <u>question</u>: Will the <u>benefits</u> of the new system be <u>greater</u> than the <u>costs</u>? If the answer is <u>yes</u> then the systems analyst will <u>recommend</u> that the new system is <u>implemented</u>. If the answer is <u>no</u> it might be worth looking for a <u>cheaper solution</u>.

2) The <u>benefits</u> are pretty much the <u>same</u> as the <u>objectives</u>.

3) The <u>costs</u> will include the costs of <u>creating</u> the new system — but there might be <u>others</u> as well. E.g. the new system might require <u>fewer workers</u> — so the firm may have to pay out <u>redundancy money</u>. Also, <u>new staff</u> may need to be <u>recruited</u> and <u>existing staff retrained</u>.

Make a <u>Recommendation</u>

1) The <u>feasibility study</u> and the <u>recommendation</u> need to be <u>presented</u> to the people who will have to <u>decide</u> whether or not to <u>proceed</u> with the new system. These are often <u>company directors</u> or <u>senior managers</u>.

2) <u>Sometimes</u> the analyst will recommend a number of <u>different solutions</u> and let the <u>others decide</u> which system to adopt.

And so I recommend that you sell off all your playing fields and give all your pupils a free laptop.

Get him off!

Do we need a colder ice box? — no, that's a freezeability study...

You won't have to produce a feasibility study for your project, but you will need to think about all the things covered on this page, especially the <u>objectives</u> of the new system. You've got to be <u>really clear</u> about the objectives for your new system before you get too involved in designing it.

Design — Input, Process, Output

This is the stage when the systems analyst really gets down to business. Make sure you know <u>what questions need to be asked</u> by the analyst — and how the <u>whole system fits together</u>.

Input — How the Data is Captured

1) The <u>input data</u> might need to be <u>organised</u> into fields of fixed or variable length.

2) The use of <u>codes</u> can <u>reduce</u> the <u>file size</u>. For example a person's <u>gender</u> can be entered as <u>M or F</u> — reducing the number of <u>bytes</u> needed to <u>store</u> the data.

3) <u>Screen forms</u> should be sketched showing what the <u>user</u> will <u>see</u> whilst they input the data.

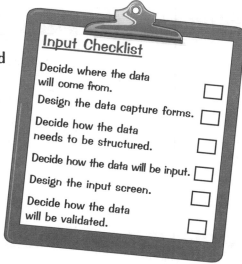

Input Checklist

Decide where the data will come from. ☐

Design the data capture forms. ☐

Decide how the data needs to be structured. ☐

Decide how the data will be input. ☐

Design the input screen. ☐

Decide how the data will be validated. ☐

Process — What Happens to It

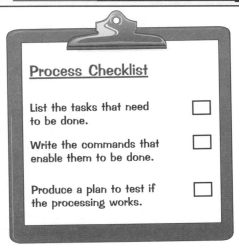

Process Checklist

List the tasks that need to be done. ☐

Write the commands that enable them to be done. ☐

Produce a plan to test if the processing works. ☐

1) The <u>tasks</u> that the system needs to perform should be based on the <u>original problem</u> and <u>objectives</u>.

2) The <u>commands</u> could include spreadsheet <u>formulas</u>, database <u>searches</u>, desktop publishing <u>page design</u>, and word-processing <u>mail-merge routines</u>.

3) The commands could also include <u>exchanging data</u> between <u>different applications</u>. For example <u>importing</u> a spreadsheet and using it to create a table in a word-processing package.

4) A <u>test plan</u> (see p. 65) for the field '<u>month of birth</u>' might include <u>typical data</u> such as <u>6</u>, <u>extreme data</u> such as <u>12</u> and <u>invalid data</u> such as <u>Boris</u>. This will test whether the <u>data validation</u> works.

Output — Let it Out

1) The <u>Golden Rule</u> is to be <u>user-friendly</u>. This means that the output must be <u>appropriate</u> for the <u>needs of the audience</u>.

2) Users should only be <u>shown</u> the information that they <u>need</u> — and it should be <u>communicated</u> in a way they will easily <u>understand</u>. <u>Layout</u> is as important as <u>content</u>.

I say old chap, could you ascertain whether my internal-combustion-engine-driven automobile possesses an erroneous vulcanised-rubber revolving device?

3) The <u>layout</u> of <u>output screens</u> and <u>printouts</u> should first be <u>sketched</u> in rough. They should then be <u>shown</u> to the <u>user</u> to <u>check</u> they are <u>OK</u>.

Output Checklist

Decide which data needs to be output. ☐

Decide how to present the information. ☐

Decide which output devices to use. ☐

Design output screens. ☐

Rubbish!

Removing a notice outside a shop — oh no, that's de-signing...

As part of the design stage of your project, you should be thinking about all the things above and recording them in your "design specification". Include sketches of input and output screens.

Design — Top-Down and Data-Flow

It's massively important to know how all the bits of the system fit together. The three diagrams on the next two pages show how this can be done. Make sure you know the differences between them.

Top-Down Diagrams Set Out the Main Tasks

1) Top-down design looks at the whole system by identifying the main tasks to be done and then breaking them down into smaller tasks.

2) If you read a top-down design from top to bottom each big task is broken down into smaller tasks. Reading it from left to right tells you the order in which they happen.

3) Top-down diagrams show what has to happen — but they don't always show how they'll happen.

4) The example below shows the tasks needed to create and print a copy of a new database record.

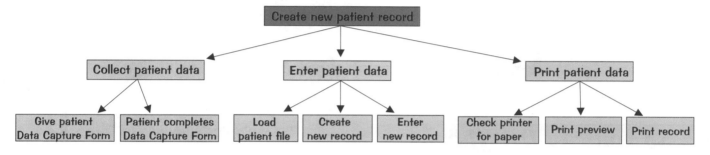

Data-Flow Diagrams Show What Happens to the Data

1) Data-flow diagrams show how data moves around the system — and what happens to it at each stage. There are three main symbols used:

An ellipse shows where data has come from. The square shows a process such as a search. The rectangle shows where the data is stored — this can include a manual store of a hard copy.

2) Data-flow diagrams show what happens to the data — but they don't show what hardware and software are needed to make this happen.

3) The example shows how an optician can send reminder letters to people who have not had an eye test within the past year.

4) This is a data-flow diagram for just one task. A whole system could be shown by linking together the separate diagrams for each task — rather like linking up different people's family trees.

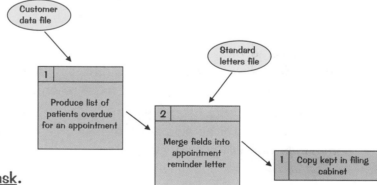

Top-down — the best feathers to fill your duvet...

Make sure you really understand how both types of diagram work. Top-down diagrams look at the whole system and break it into smaller chunks. Data-flow diagrams show how data will move through the system, they don't include the hardware or software involved.

Design — System Flow Charts

Most people find these incredibly <u>scary</u>. But they're pretty straightforward really.
Once you know what the symbols mean all you've got to do is practise <u>drawing</u> them.

Learn the Symbols...

System flow charts are similar to data-flow diagrams but more detailed (just look at all the symbols).
They include the <u>hardware</u> the system will use and also use <u>decision boxes</u> (see the example below).

The <u>symbol</u> for <u>stored data</u> is sometimes
<u>replaced</u> by one of the <u>other magenta</u>
<u>symbols</u> if the analyst wants to <u>specify</u> the
type of <u>storage medium</u> to be used.
(The colours used here aren't standard,
they're just to make it easier to follow.)

I see a tall dark wardrobe,
and lots of shelf space...

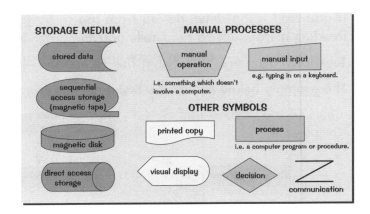

...So you can Use Them

1) Here's an <u>example</u> of a system flow chart for
   creating a <u>new patient record</u> at a dentist's surgery.

2) The customer completes a <u>data-capture form</u>.
   This information is then <u>entered</u> onto
   the patient record file <u>by the receptionist</u>.

3) The new patient record is then <u>used to create a</u>
   <u>mail-merged letter</u> welcoming the new patient to the surgery.

4) The decision box is an example of an <u>algorithm</u>.
   If the input data is invalid the receptionist
   must <u>verify</u> whether the input data is the
   same as the data on the original data-capture form.

5) If it's the same then the patient needs to be contacted
   to check the correct details. If it's different there has been
   an <u>input error</u> and the receptionist must re-enter the data.

6) <u>Once the flow chart's been drawn</u>,
   the programmer will be able write the
   commands that will <u>create the system</u>.

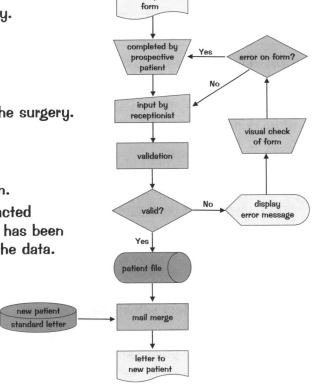

"Algorithm"...."No Ted, he'll be fine on his own"...

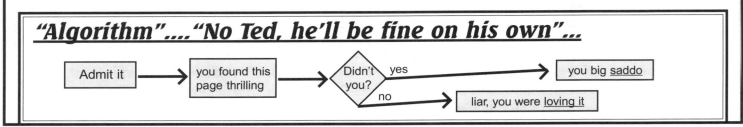

Testing and User Documentation

A system is tested both during building and after it's built. You need to know what tests are done and why. It'd also help to know the different types of documentation that need to be written.

The New System Needs to be Fully Tested

The new system must be fully tested to see if the design has worked.
One way is to use test data — there are three types:

> Normal data — anything that the programmer knows should work in the system.
> Invalid data — anything the programmer knows that the system should reject.
> Extreme data — data at the edges of the expected data range. E.g. if a database field
> contains exam results out of 80, you'd test it with values 0 and 80.

Any part of the system that doesn't work is said to have a bug — testing enables the programmer to know which parts of the system need to be debugged.

User Documentation Explains How to Operate the System

User guides are written to help the people who will be using the system.

A Basic User Guide Should Include...

1) How to open the software
2) How to open files
3) How to enter data into the system
4) How to obtain outputs (on paper or screen)
5) How to save changes
6) How to close and exit the system

User guides need to be written in simple language so the users can understand what they have to do. Using lots of annotated screenshots helps to make things much clearer.

A Systems Analyst would also produce technical documentation written for the computer engineers and programmers who will maintain the system after it's been installed. You won't need to do this for your ICT system, but you should produce a development diary instead...

1) A development diary is a list of what you did in creating the system. You can do it as a list of dated entries or a list of sessions.

2) Whichever you choose, you must make sure that someone could reproduce your work from reading your development diary.

3) The two key things it should include are:
   - technical descriptions of what you did
   - screen dumps that show the result of the work you've described.

#lprint !<>"large" NOR{/n $%^"butt"}*273; — ha ha ha...

You need to be thinking about how you're going to test your system even at the design stage — you should put together a full test plan which you can then carry out when your system is all set up. And remember, if you want top marks, you need to test the whole system, not just bits of it.

Implementation and Evaluation

Implementation happens when <u>data</u> from the old system is <u>loaded onto the new system</u> — so the new system is <u>ready for use</u>.

There are Three Different Ways to Implement the System

You probably won't actually have to install the system you've created in the business, but you should know the different ways that it <u>could be</u> done by a systems analyst...

1) <u>Direct implementation</u> is when the old system is <u>decommissioned</u> and the new system <u>started up</u> at the <u>same time</u>. There is <u>no change-over period</u> so the users need to be able to use the new system straight away.

 An <u>advantage</u> is that the <u>benefits</u> of the new system happen <u>as quickly as possible</u>.

 A <u>disadvantage</u> is that any <u>bugs</u> not picked up during testing could have <u>disastrous effects</u>.

2) <u>Phased implementation</u> is when <u>different parts</u> of the system are <u>introduced one at a time</u>. The <u>old system</u> is <u>kept running</u> while this happens.

 A <u>plus</u> point is that the <u>new system</u> has <u>time</u> to be <u>fully tested</u> — so <u>fewer problems</u> should occur.

 A <u>snag</u> is that it can take a long time <u>to introduce</u> the new system this way — so the <u>benefits</u> take a <u>long time</u> to come through.

3) <u>Parallel implementation</u> is when the <u>new system</u> is introduced <u>all in one go</u> — but the <u>old system</u> is <u>kept running</u> whilst the new one is tested. This means that for a while there are <u>two systems</u>.

 A <u>benefit</u> is that the new system can be <u>tested very quickly</u> — and <u>problems</u> can be sorted out <u>without</u> important operations being affected.

 A <u>problem</u> is that all <u>tasks</u> need to be <u>done twice</u>.

Evaluation Checks if the System Still Meets its Objectives

1) Once the system is installed its performance will be <u>monitored</u> to see whether it's working properly. From time to time it'll be <u>evaluated</u>. This is a check to <u>see if the system still meets its objectives</u> — in other words whether it still does what it was designed to do.

2) <u>Evaluation</u> is basically <u>repeating</u> the <u>research carried out at the start</u> of the system's life cycle. In other words <u>observing</u> and <u>interviewing</u> users and <u>studying</u> printouts.

3) One reason why the system might <u>not</u> meet its objectives is if the <u>workload increases</u>. The <u>demands</u> on the system may become <u>greater than</u> its <u>ability</u> to cope. In other words it becomes <u>obsolete</u>. This brings the system life cycle <u>full circle</u> and the analyst is brought back to begin work on a <u>new system</u>.

My evaluation — systems analysis ~~really sucks~~ is great!

As far as your project is concerned, evaluation will basically involve looking at the system you've created, <u>comparing</u> it to all those nice <u>objectives</u> you made and deciding if it's worked. Has your new system overcome all the problems of the old system? Don't be afraid to be critical of your own system. Examiners like this kind of thing if you can <u>explain why</u> bits of it haven't worked so well.

Section 2.3 — Revision Summary

Well done — you made it to the end of Section 2.3. You're almost ready to go off and do your own project. Before you do, go over these questions here. They'll help you check you've learnt everything from the section. They may be less exciting than an economy bag of potatoes, but hey...

1) What is your name? Sorry, only kidding. What comes between identifying a problem with an existing computer system and building a new system to replace it?

2) Suggest why an old computer system might need replacing.

3) List three ways of gathering information about the performance of an old system.

4) What is the difference between objectives, performance criteria and evaluation criteria?

5) What does a cost-benefit study do?

6) List three things that should be done when designing a system's inputs.

7) List three things that should be done when designing a system's processes.

8) List three things that should be done when designing a system's outputs.

9) In which two ways do you read a top-down diagram?

10) What does it mean if you see a square on a data-flow diagram?
   a) Input   b) Process   c) Store.

11) Correctly label each symbol in the box.

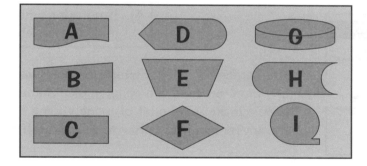

12) Which would be the correct symbol for each of the following events:
   a) A screen prompt to log on
   b) Keying in your user name
   c) The computer checking that your user name is on its list
   d) A hard copy of your filenames

13) What are the three types of test data needed? Give an example for each if testing the validation of data entries for the field "Day of month born".

14) Give four things that a basic user guide should include.

15) Explain how parallel implementation is different from direct implementation.

16) Explain how phased implementation is different from parallel implementation.

17) Give one benefit and one problem of each type of implementation.

18) What is the difference between monitoring and evaluation?

Online Shopping and Auctions

Online shopping and auctions are becoming more and more popular with businesses and customers. This page is about how this has affected the world of business.

Loads of People Buy Stuff Online

Apparently, in 2004, 1 in 10 of all credit card transactions took place online. That might not sound like much, but think about how many purchases it must be. Here's why it's good and not so good:

Good Stuff About Internet Shopping

1) It's more convenient being able to buy everything you want from the comfort of your own home, especially if you find it difficult to get out of the house.

2) Online 'Internet only' prices are often lower because less staff are needed in a warehouse than in a normal shop.

3) Because the Internet is global, you get much more choice shopping online. Internet shops can reach anyone in the world who has a web browser.

Not so Good Stuff About Internet Shopping

1) Not being able to see and handle the goods means they might not be what you really wanted, and it can be harder to get your money back if they're dodgy.

2) It can take a while to receive what you've bought — not much use for that emergency present.

3) Because Internet shops need less workers, there are fewer retail jobs as it becomes more popular. Some smaller retailers without the money or skills for ICT systems are going out of business.

4) If you don't have a computer then you miss out on cheaper online goods.

You can sell or auction stuff you don't want any more on sites like ebay.co.uk. Some people make quite a bit of money doing this. It's environmentally better to re-use stuff too.

Online Shopping Affects Businesses

There are advantages for businesses who sell online:

1) If you only sell online, you don't need to spend money renting a shop or employing so many staff. This means you reduce your costs and can charge less for your product, which should mean you get more customers.

2) Your business is available to people 24 hours a day, not just during normal shop opening times.

3) Because the Internet is available world-wide, you can reach people in countries you haven't even heard of, let alone thought about selling in.

There are disadvantages for some businesses though. For example, lots of smallish high street shops are going bust because they can't compete with the likes of Amazon and other online giants.

Careful — one false click and you'll buy a Darius album...

So there you go... Online shopping is out there. You can buy pretty much anything online, from pretty much anywhere in the world. Good for you, and good for the guys who want to sell you stuff. The thing is, though, it really takes the fun out of shopping. Well, if you like that sort of thing.

Other Online Services

The Internet isn't only used by organisations to sell stuff — there are many other <u>services</u> out there.

It's Easy to Book Holidays Online

Not long ago, people would just go to a travel agent and book a '<u>package holiday</u>'.
This is where the travel agent <u>arranges</u> everything — flights, travel from the airport, your hotel, etc.
So you don't have to organise anything yourself apart from paying the travel agent.

Nowadays though, loads of <u>websites</u> let you arrange all the separate parts of a holiday <u>yourself</u> — flights, hotel rooms, train tickets etc. So you don't have to settle for what the travel agent offers.

> It's often a lot <u>cheaper</u> to book holidays online. There are loads of <u>budget airlines</u> like Ryanair which are almost exclusively Internet only. They sell really <u>cheap flights</u>.

A bit of a webpage from www.lastminute.com

Websites Offer Free Services

Some websites offer <u>free services</u> in the hope that once you're on their website, you'll spend <u>money</u> on their products or services.

1) Websites that let you book <u>holidays</u> online often offer free <u>tourist information</u>, 'virtual visits' to places and even maps.

2) Websites trying to sell car insurance, breakdown service membership and car-related products sometimes offer a free <u>route-planning</u> service. You type in where you're going from and to, and it tells you exactly how to get there by car.

3) Websites that sell <u>train</u> tickets will let you find out what <u>times</u> the trains are.

Other websites provide free services, but have lots of <u>adverts</u> on them.
This is how they make <u>money</u> — companies pay them to put their adverts on the website.
Free web-based e-mail, chat rooms, message boards and news services all have adverts on them.

> Some websites do exist solely to provide you with a service for <u>free</u>.
> *   For example, <u>NHS Direct</u> gives out free <u>health advice</u> and has a special questionnaire which helps you diagnose your own illness.
> *   Your <u>bank</u> will have an online service which lets you make payments and transfer funds whenever you like.

Websites Offer Services with a Cost too

Obviously, there are loads of services on the Internet that <u>aren't free</u>. Here's a few...
Dating agencies, employment agencies, people finders etc...

Careful — Kingston in Jamaica, or Kingston upon Thames?

Ooh, what a big page with so many facts. Well, if you've ever been on the Internet I'm sure you know it all already. The simple fact is that there's loads of really <u>useful stuff</u> out there on the net, some of it you have to pay for, and some you don't. Nothing new there.

Online Banking

Not everyone has time to get to the bank when it's open, and some people don't like queuing in the bank even if they have the time. Online banking has the answers to these problems and more.

Bank Accounts are Easy to Access Online

1) To be able to access your bank account via the Internet, you need to register with the bank, who will send you a passcode through the post.

2) You need security information to access your account. This is in case anyone else uses your computer, or if you access your account from a public computer. You need to give information like your date of birth, address and postcode as well as your passcode.

3) While you're logged in, you're accessing the website through an encrypted connection, which means that the information passing back and forth can't be hacked into by anyone else.

There are lots of Bank Services Online

Most of the things you can do at your bank, you can also do using online banking:

1) You can transfer money from one account to another.

2) You can check your balance.

3) You can apply for a loan.

4) You can set up standing orders or cancel direct debits (payments for bills that come out of your account automatically on certain days of the month).

There are a few things you can't do online though, like paying in money.

In the future, only weirdy people will be banking in the street.

There are Advantages and Disadvantages for the Banks

Advantages for Banks

1) Online banking is really useful for the bank's customers. Keeping the customers happy is important if the bank is to make any money.

2) Less staff are needed, which reduces costs — small branches can even be closed altogether.

3) Paper costs are lower.

4) Less storage space is needed.

Disadvantages for Banks

1) A high level of security is needed, which is expensive.

2) You can never guarantee that security systems are totally secure. If anybody hacked in and got hold of customer details, the bank would be in a lot of trouble.

3) It's quite expensive to set up an on-line service.

4) If branch closures happen, the bank might lose customers.

Remember that if branches close to save banks money, people will lose their jobs — which is never a good thing for individuals and communities.

Since I've had the Internet I've done a lot more banking...

Online banking is one of the most useful things the Internet has to offer. Well, that's my opinion anyway. (The opinion of a person who lives miles and miles from a bank, and couldn't get to it when it's open without pulling a sickie, which would put at risk the chance of having money anyway...)

Technical Support and Databases

As ICT gets used more in business, more and more <u>IT support</u> is needed to help people using it.

Organisations Provide Technical Support and Services

Some places of work have so many computers that they employ a special team of IT people to sort stuff out. Other places don't have IT people so they need to call someone in from time to time.

1) Businesses often need help setting up and looking after a <u>network</u>. Places like schools might have a network, but won't want to employ someone full-time to look after it. They'll call in a <u>network technician</u> whenever something needs to be done.

2) Businesses might also pay a company to <u>host</u> their <u>website</u>. <u>Hosting</u> means having the website stored on a computer that's always connected to the Internet. This computer will have some special software to make the website secure, such as a <u>firewall</u>. It's often cheaper to buy <u>hosting</u> than to buy your own <u>server</u> and have that connected to the Internet all the time.

Security Companies Protect your Computer

<u>Security</u> companies do their best to stop <u>viruses</u>, <u>trojans</u> and <u>hackers</u>:

1) In order to protect your business from attack from hackers or viruses, you might pay an IT security company to install software to protect your <u>network</u> or <u>website</u>.

2) This software will mainly be a <u>virus scanner</u> and <u>firewall</u>. It's important to have both. A <u>firewall</u> protects from hackers, and a <u>virus scanner</u> protects against <u>viruses and trojans</u>.

Barbara couldn't see the big deal about having trojans around the office.

Databases Need to be Customised

<u>Databases</u> are widely used in business. It's quite common for companies to hire someone to create a <u>customised</u> database that exactly fits their business needs. It's also quite common for people to be employed specially to create and <u>maintain</u> databases.

There are two kinds of <u>customised database</u> that you should know about:

Analytical Databases	Operational Databases
(Also known as OLAP — On Line Analytic Processing)	(Also known as OLTP — On Line Transaction Processing)
These databases let you look at data, but not change it. e.g.	These databases are meant to be changed a lot over time — possibly lots of times a day. e.g.
• Catalogues (like on Amazon.co.uk)	• Warehouse stock control (see page 44)
• Historical data (like populations or births, deaths and marriages)	• Customer order tracking
• Past sales data	

I customised my database — now it matches my shoes...

Right, well that was a fairly <u>boring</u> page wasn't it? IT people do some stuff, make computers work, yeah yeah, blah blah. Databases need looking after, whatever, blah blah. OK, I know it's boring, especially databases, but just read it and <u>learn it</u> and make sure it stays in your head.

ICT in Call Centres

For large businesses that don't have offices or shops all over the country, one of the ways they can communicate with their customers is by having a <u>call centre</u>.

Lots of Big Businesses Have Call Centres

1) Some organisations receive thousands of calls a day, so it makes sense to send all the calls to the same <u>place</u> with the same <u>phone number</u> rather than having lots of different numbers.

2) A call centre is simply a building with lots of employees who <u>call people</u> or <u>answer the phone</u>.

3) They use a <u>computerised</u> phone system with a <u>headset earpiece</u> and <u>microphone</u>.

4) Having call centres means that you can <u>train</u> staff to answer the phone, so they're really good at <u>customer service</u> and know the answers to frequently asked questions.

5) Often, large businesses from this country have their call centres in <u>India</u> and other places where labour is fairly <u>cheap</u>. When you phone, you normally won't realise that you're talking to India.

Although call centre operators are trained to deal with simple queries, they may struggle to deal with more specific ones. Customers can be passed from one operator to another, which is very frustrating.

Call Centres Can't Work Without ICT

Call centres rely on ICT to work properly. Here are three ways in which call centres use ICT:

Call Routing

<u>Call routing</u> is when you have to press a certain number to get through to a certain department ('press 1 if you have a bill enquiry, press 2 if you...'). It usually only works if you have a <u>touch-tone</u> phone (one that makes a noise when you press the keys), as the computer recognises the tone of each number you press.

Sound Recorders

Your voice, and the voice of the person you speak to, will often be recorded digitally, through a program similar to <u>Sound Recorder</u> on your PC. This is done so that the conversation can be listened to again and <u>evaluated</u> so that the people working at the call centre can get better at their jobs.

Queues

If the call centre is busy, you'll probably be placed in a <u>queue</u>. The organisation will need an <u>ICT</u> system to manage this queue, and to connect the next person in line. You'll also often hear a recorded message telling you which number you are in the queue.

Call centres... bleugh.

Call centres... Urgh, don't get me started on call centres. The usual is to be held in a queue for half an hour listening to Robbie Williams in <u>panpipes</u>, only to get through to somebody who then puts you through to somebody else and then yet another person who still can't answer your simple question.

ICT in Advertising and Marketing

Wherever you look these days there's usually someone waiting to <u>sell</u> you something. ICT has made this even harder to avoid.

ICT has made Advertising Easier and More Effective

ICT has made it easier and cheaper to produce really effective eye-catching advertising:

1) These days, using fairly cheap computer <u>equipment</u>, it is really easy to produce a professional looking magazine advert or poster. Anybody with basic training could use the <u>software</u>.

2) <u>Graphics</u> are easier to work with, meaning that more eye-catching and imaginative <u>images</u> can be used to draw your attention to an advert.

3) If there are <u>people</u> featured in the advert, they can be made to <u>look better</u> using graphics software. For example, you can remove spots and wrinkles from their faces.

4) Technology is now so advanced that <u>special effects</u> can be used in **TV** adverts. You can even get completely computer-animated adverts on **TV** that look as good as fairly recent films.

> Annoyingly enough, ICT has also made it easier for people to call you up to try and sell you <u>double-glazing</u>. They now have huge <u>databases</u> which contain thousands of peoples' phone numbers instead of having to look through the phone book for people to call.

ICT has Created New Forms of Advertising

Thanks to ICT, there are many new ways of advertisers targeting you. If you ever go on the <u>Internet</u>, you're not going to get away from the piles and piles of adverts hunting you down.

1) <u>Pop-up advertising</u> is when the web page you're looking at opens a new window containing an advert. If you <u>click</u> on the window, it'll take you to a web page where you can buy what they're advertising.

2) Pop-up adverts are really <u>annoying</u> as they get in the way of the web page you're looking at. You can get <u>pop-up blocking software</u> to stop these adverts appearing.

3) Some websites have <u>banner adverts</u>. These are part of the page you're reading, so they don't get in the way so much. If you <u>click</u> on them you'll get to another web page.

4) If you have an e-mail address, you'll probably get e-mails from people or companies offering you products or services. If you didn't ask for these emails, they're known as <u>spam</u>.

5) It's now <u>against the law</u> to send spam, and companies can be fined for doing so.

Now here's the most important thing on the page. Don't forget this. Your exam will be...

Annoying Pop-up Advert

Ever wanted a naked statue of yourself? Just click on:

www.nakedstatuesofyou.com

Click on www.cgpbooks.co.uk for more great books...

Funny this, it's basically a page about how ICT has made the world much more <u>annoying</u> for normal people like us. It's great for <u>companies</u> who want you to know about their stuff, but I don't want to know. And I don't want a Russian bride, or a fake university degree, or cheap Viagra either, thank you.

Section 3.1 — Revision Summary

That's all there is to learn in this section. Phew. Well, it's not quite over properly until you've had a go at some questions. Don't worry, they're not too hard, and if you can't do them just look back at the right pages, cos the answers are all there somewhere.

1) Out of all credit card transactions in 2004, what ratio took place online?

2) What kind of website can you use to sell items to other people through?

3) What kind of reasons do people have for not shopping online?

4) What kind of free services might a travel website contain to try to attract customers?

5) List four holiday-related things you can book online.

6) What free services are offered on the Internet? List another four.

7 a) What kind of security information do you need to provide to access your bank account online?

  b) And what do the bank send you through the post to go along with this information?

8) List four things you can do through online banking.

9) Give two reasons why a bank would want to provide online access for customers.

10) Name one technical service that might be provided for a business by an outside organisation.

11) Name something you might use an analytical database for.

12) Name something you might use an operational database for.

13) Why might a business have a call centre?

14) Name three uses of ICT systems in a call centre.

15) What effects has ICT technology had on TV advertising?

16) Explain how graphics software might be used to alter images used in a magazine advert for a new beauty product.

17) How do phone salespeople find your number nowadays?

18) What form of Internet advertising can be blocked?

19) What form of Internet advertising forms part of a web page?

20) What is spam?

ICT in the Workplace

ICT is changing the <u>types of jobs</u> that people are employed to do, and how they perform them.

ICT has Replaced Some Jobs but Created Others

Computers have completely <u>replaced</u> humans in performing some jobs, and <u>reduced</u> the number of people needed to do others. But the need to <u>build and operate computers</u> has resulted in new jobs being <u>created</u> and new industries <u>emerging</u>. Below are a few examples:

JOBS BEING REPLACED BY COMPUTERS	JOBS BEING CREATED BY COMPUTERS
1) <u>Manufacturing jobs</u> — many workers are replaced by a few highly trained workers manning automated workstations.	1) Computer hardware <u>designers</u> and <u>manufacturers</u>.
2) <u>Bank</u> and <u>retail jobs</u> — replaced by computer systems and online shopping.	2) <u>Systems analysts</u> and <u>programmers</u> to design systems and write software.
3) <u>Traditional office jobs</u>, e.g. filing clerks and typists, replaced by computer systems.	3) <u>Network managers</u> and <u>IT technicians</u> to maintain computer systems.
	4) <u>Website designers</u>.

ICT is increasingly used by All Workers

<u>Workers</u> in general, and particularly those in <u>office jobs</u>, are being required to spend <u>more and more</u> of their working day <u>using computers</u>. This has <u>pros</u> and <u>cons</u> for both employers and employees:

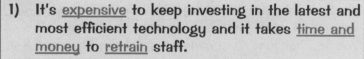

PROS

1) Employers benefit because computers can <u>increase</u> the amount of work done. This makes businesses more <u>productive</u> and so more <u>competitive</u>.

2) Workers benefit if computers can do the boring, <u>repetitive</u> work and leave them to do the <u>interesting</u> jobs.

CONS

1) It's <u>expensive</u> to keep investing in the latest and most efficient technology and it takes <u>time and money</u> to <u>retrain</u> staff.

2) There may be <u>job losses</u> as <u>computers replace people</u> for some tasks, such as car-assembly.

ICT Can Affect the Way People Communicate

ICT has made <u>communication</u> easier, faster and more reliable (usually). This is great news for businesses, especially those who need to communicate regularly with other organisations or offices <u>overseas</u>. <u>E-mail</u> in particular is cheap, fast, can be sent with <u>attachments</u>, and the same information can be sent to lots of people at once. The person doesn't need to be at their desk to receive the information, as it will wait in their <u>inbox</u> until they check their e-mail.

However, there is a downside. Because e-mail is so convenient, it is often <u>over-used</u>. Staff can end up spending a significant amount of their working time reading and responding to e-mails. They might be <u>slow to respond</u> to important communications because they're too busy with e-mails that <u>aren't</u> really relevant to them. So although e-mail can help make everything quicker and easier, it can also end up making some staff <u>less productive</u>. How ironic.

They'll never replace ME — couldn't get a computer that lazy...

Advances in ICT have led to a lot of changes in the <u>way people work</u> and the <u>jobs they do</u>. As with anything new, some people <u>benefited</u> from the changes and other people <u>lost out</u>. Make sure <u>you</u> benefit by learning all the stuff on this page about changes, advantages and disadvantages.

ICT in the Workplace

Over the past couple of decades, ICT has become more and more widely used in the workplace. This has had a big effect on employee work patterns. It hasn't all been good news, either...

ICT Has Changed Where People Work

TELEWORKING

1) ICT developments like the Internet, e-mail, mobile phones, fax, etc. mean employees can now telework (i.e. work from home), instead of travelling in to an office each day.

2) Teleworking reduces the amount of office space needed, which lowers costs for employers. There are also advantages for employees, for example:

   • Less time and money taken up by travelling to work.
   • Often allows more flexible hours.
   • Ideal for disabled workers, and for those who have to care for young children.

3) But there are also disadvantages — it's harder for employers to make sure confidential information is protected. Disadvantages for employees include:

   • They can feel isolated and lonely because of the lack of personal contact with colleagues.
   • There is no clear separation of work and home life, which some people find stressful.
   • There are often more distractions at home, e.g. housework, children.

HOT-DESKING

ICT has even changed where people work inside the office. Many workers today don't have their own desk, filing cabinet, etc., as they would have in the past. If networks are used, and hours are flexible, they can sit at any desk and still have access (over the network) to everything they need to do their job. So many organisations now use hot-desking, where people arriving at work just pick any desk that's free. This saves the organisation money, because they can use smaller offices and less equipment.

E-mail, Mobiles and Laptops make Workers Easy to Contact

1) ICT technology such as e-mail, mobile phones and laptops makes it much easier to get hold of people when they're not at work. Below are a few points to think about:

   • People can use laptops, mobile phones, etc. to work while travelling.
   • Employees can be contacted about work at any time, including outside working hours.
   • People can easily finish off work at home on their laptops.

2) This is good for the business as staff are more productive, which makes more money. Employees can be easily contacted in an work-related emergency, or if extra tasks need doing.

3) However, it's not always good for staff. It might be to their advantage if they can catch up on work at home and spend their time usefully when travelling, but often it just leads to more time spent working with no increase in pay. Their private lives can be interrupted at any time by work demands, and they might suffer from extra stress.

Dah dah der dah, dah dah der dah — HELLO? I'M ON THE TRAIN, BOSS!

Imagine if your teachers kept ringing you up on your mobile to ask you physics and history questions outside school time. Pretty annoying, I'd say. So although ICT has made work better in a lot of ways, it also potentially allows bosses to take advantage of their employees. Bummer.

ICT in the Workplace

ICT is getting more and more important in the workplace, but it's also constantly <u>changing</u> and developing. This means it's essential that staff get the training they need to keep their skills <u>up to date</u>.

Staff May Need ICT <u>Qualifications</u> or Special Training

1) Many employers today choose new staff at least partly based on whether they have ICT <u>qualifications</u>, like a GCSE or the <u>European Computer Driving Licence (ECDL)</u>. Existing staff might be expected to study for and achieve these qualifications.

Dolphin training.
(Looks prettier than ICT training.)

2) Nationally recognised qualifications like these cover the applications that are most commonly used in <u>offices</u> — things like <u>word processing</u>, <u>databases</u> and <u>spreadsheets</u>, as well as using <u>e-mail</u> and the <u>Internet</u>.

3) But lots of companies need their staff to be able to use different, <u>specialist</u> computer programmes and equipment. These companies then need to provide <u>specialist training</u>. Some companies use one of the <u>developers</u> of the software or equipment to teach an employee how to use it. This person can then be used to train other members of staff.

4) This type of training, where the trainer works for the company, is called <u>in-house training</u>. It's useful because it means that the skills people learn are the <u>exact ones</u> that they'll need to do their job. On the other hand, somebody experienced has to stop doing their usual job so that they can be responsible for learning about the equipment and training others.

5) Sometimes employees need training that can't be provided within the company they work for. They might have to go to a <u>college</u> or special centre. This is known as <u>off-the-job training</u>.

ICT Can Play an Important Part in <u>Training Staff</u>

1) Organisations <u>benefit</u> from keeping their staff up to date with the latest ICT advances. New technology can help <u>save time</u> and make employees more <u>productive</u>.

2) However, it's <u>expensive</u> to train staff and keep them up to date, so smaller companies can miss out. This is where <u>ICT</u> can be handy in training people in how to use ICT. Crazy. For example:

ICT can be used for more than just playing games, you know.

- The <u>Internet</u> can be a good source of training materials. It's more convenient than sending staff to an outside centre.
- Interactive <u>CD-ROMs</u> on a variety of ICT topics can be bought for use by employees. Staff can work through them alone, so there's no need for other staff to teach them.
- ICT technology can be used by companies to create their <u>own</u> training resources. These can be <u>specially tailored</u> to the tasks that employees need to know about.

3) ICT can also be used to <u>monitor</u> staff performance and to carry out computer-based <u>assessments</u>. This can help the company identify when their staff need more training, and what type of training they should be doing.

The ECDL can be tricky — especially the reverse park...

<u>Good news</u> for you then — <u>lots of businesses</u> like to employ people with an <u>ICT qualification</u>. Which is what you're learning all this boring stuff about learning boring stuff for. One day it could well land you your <u>dream job</u>. Footballers, pop stars — they all need <u>Applied ICT GCSE</u>, you know.

ICT and the Law

Computers are increasingly used to <u>store and process important data</u>.
It's very <u>easy</u> to <u>transfer data electronically</u> — so there are <u>laws</u> to control computer use.

The Data Protection Act controls the Use of Personal Data

1) The <u>Data Protection Act</u> was introduced in the UK in 1984. It gives rights to <u>data subjects</u> (i.e. people who have data about them stored on computer systems). The Act was updated in 1998 to take the increasing use of computers, and changes in European Union law, into account.

2) The Act mainly consists of <u>eight</u> data protection <u>principles</u> — summarised here ➡➡➡➡➡➡

3) The law entitles data subjects to <u>see the personal data</u> about them that's held by an organisation. If an organisation <u>breaks the law</u>, they can be fined and made to pay <u>compensation</u> to the data subject.

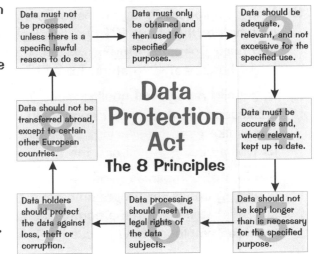

Data must not be processed unless there is a specific lawful reason to do so.

Data must only be obtained and then used for specified purposes.

Data should be adequate, relevant, and not excessive for the specified use.

Data must be accurate and, where relevant, kept up to date.

Data should not be kept longer than is necessary for the specified purpose.

Data processing should meet the legal rights of the data subjects.

Data holders should protect the data against loss, theft or corruption.

Data should not be transferred abroad, except to certain other European countries.

Data Protection Act — The 8 Principles

The Computer Misuse Act prevents Illegal Access to Files

This law was introduced in 1990 to cope with the problems of computer <u>hackers</u> and <u>viruses</u>. The Act made the following <u>three things illegal</u>:

1) <u>Unauthorised access</u> to <u>computer material</u> (e.g. <u>hacking</u>). This includes viewing parts of a network you're not permitted to see, and the illegal copying of programs — <u>software piracy</u>.

2) Gaining <u>unauthorised access</u> to a computer to carry out serious <u>crimes</u> like <u>fraud</u> and <u>blackmail</u>.

3) <u>Unauthorised changing</u> of computer files — including <u>planting viruses</u>, and <u>deleting files</u>.

If convicted, the offender can face an unlimited fine and a five-year prison sentence.

The Copyright, Design and Patents Act controls Illegal Copying

This law was introduced in 1989, and makes it <u>illegal to copy a file without permission</u> from the <u>owner</u> or <u>copyright holder</u>. Individuals and organisations who break this law risk an <u>unlimited</u> fine.

There are <u>three ways</u> that the law is often broken:

1) <u>Using software</u> without the proper <u>licence</u>. So if you have a licence to use a word processor on one <u>stand-alone</u> computer, but you then install it on all the machines in a <u>network</u>, you're breaking the law.

2) <u>Downloading</u> text or images <u>from the Internet</u> and <u>using</u> them without saying where you got them, or without receiving the copyright owner's <u>permission</u>.

3) <u>Copying</u> a computer program you use at work and running it on a computer at home, without <u>permission</u> from the copyright holder.

I turned my PC into a fishtank — is that computer misuse...

<u>Chat up line number 143</u>: *Hey, did you know — the Copyright, Design and Patents Act of 1989 made it illegal to copy a file without permission. Fancy going out tonight...*
For <u>each law</u>, you should know <u>what it is</u>, what <u>protection</u> it offers, and what <u>area of ICT</u> it affects.

ICT and the Law

A few more <u>laws</u> for you to learn about on this page. Not exactly thrilling, but quite important.

The Health and Safety at Work Act was Passed in 1974

1) This law was passed to ensure that people would be as <u>safe</u> as possible at work.

2) It states that employers have to take <u>reasonable steps</u> to ensure the health, safety and welfare of their employees at work. This might include providing safe <u>premises</u> and <u>systems of work</u>, and making their employees aware of health and safety information.

3) The Act also states that <u>employees</u> have a responsibility to use equipment correctly, to protect colleagues and customers, and to make their employer aware of any problems.

Health and Safety Regulations (1992) Protect VDU Users

The main law covering computer use at work is the <u>Health and Safety (Display Screen Equipment) Regulations 1992</u>. The law says that employers need to do <u>five main things</u>:

1) Make sure that computer equipment (and the area around it) is <u>safe</u>.

2) Provide certain things, e.g. proper computer <u>chairs</u> and good <u>lighting</u>.

3) Allow <u>regular</u> breaks or allow employees to do <u>non-computer</u> work.

4) Provide <u>free eye tests</u> to all staff who regularly use VDUs at work.

5) Provide health and safety training and information.

The Government is Allowed to Monitor Communication

1) <u>The Regulations of Investigatory Powers Act (2000)</u> defines the powers the government has to access communications like telephone conversations, e-mails, etc.

2) These powers are needed to collect evidence against <u>criminals</u>, or for <u>national security</u>.

3) However, some people are worried that the Act gives the government too much power — they're allowed to target <u>anyone</u>, not just criminal suspects. They can monitor phone calls and use of the Internet of people just in case they catch someone doing something wrong.

Organisations May Follow Other Regulations

1) There are various <u>EU regulations</u> controlling computer use, and many organisations follow these, even though they're not yet law in the UK.

2) There are also <u>Internet Codes of Practice (ICOPs)</u>. The <u>Internet</u> isn't owned by anyone, and people are <u>free</u> to put what they like on it. But ICOPs exist as <u>guidelines</u> for everyone involved in the Internet.

3) They cover things like giving a <u>warning</u> about pages that might offend people, making sure <u>children's sites</u> are suitable for children, and checking Internet adverts are <u>honest</u>.

People can put what they like on the Internet. Unfortunately.

Big brother is watching you...

That's a cultural reference to the <u>classic</u> George Orwell novel '1984', not to a reality TV show... just wanted to make that clear. I think reality TV trash like that is <u>melting</u> the brains of the entire nation. Hmm, what time is Celebrity Strictly Come Dancing on... think I'm going to have to tape the X factor.

Problems Created by ICT

ICT has brought about <u>changes</u> in business, entertainment, communication, work, and many other areas of everyday life. Mostly these changes have been <u>positive</u>, but ICT does have its <u>drawbacks</u>.

The Internet Has Made it Easier to Commit Fraud

1) <u>Internet shopping</u> (page 68) is very popular, but people still have doubts over its security. <u>Credit card</u> details should always be <u>encrypted</u>, but some people worry that a clever hacker could still intercept them.

2) The Internet is also used to defraud people via <u>web scams</u>. Common web scams include getting people to pay for goods which never arrive, getting web-users to contribute to non-existent <u>charities</u>, and persuading people to hand over their bank details as part of '<u>get rich quick</u>' schemes (but then simply <u>emptying</u> the accounts instead).

3) ICT can be used to commit other kinds of <u>fraud</u> too, e.g. a recent scam has involved criminals attaching hidden <u>devices</u> to ATMs (cash machines) which scan people's cards and can be used to create replicas. These replicas are then used to empty people's accounts. Scary stuff.

There Are Worries About Misuse of Personal Information

1) Some websites on the Internet can drop a '<u>cookie</u>' onto your computer, which lets them <u>identify</u> you and find out what other websites you have visited. This is useful for companies, because they can find out what sort of things you're interested in and what you've been buying. But some people think it's an invasion of <u>privacy</u>.

2) People are always handing over <u>personal information</u> on the Internet, e.g. when entering competitions, booking flights or finding insurance. But some companies pass or sell on this information <u>without</u> permission. This is against the <u>Data Protection Act</u>, but it can be hard to find out who's responsible, and the victim might not even know it's happened.

There Are Three Other Common Concerns About ICT Misuse

① **Chatrooms** There have been concerns about the <u>safety</u> of using <u>chatrooms</u>, especially for young people. Chatrooms are sites on the Internet where people can have typed <u>conversations</u>. But you can't tell who you're <u>really</u> talking to, and whether they're telling the truth about themselves. There could be potentially <u>dangerous</u> people using your chatroom, so you should <u>never</u> give out personal details like your address or phone number, or arrange to meet someone.

② **Viruses** A <u>virus</u> is a computer programme that has been designed to cause <u>damage</u> to the system it infects. They can be <u>spread</u> via e-mails or through networks, and many are able to <u>copy</u> themselves automatically and spread to other computers. Viruses can cost both home users and organisations a lot of <u>money</u> and <u>distress</u>.

③ **Spam** This is like junk mail, but it's a <u>junk e-mail</u> which can be sent to thousands or millions of users at once. As well as being annoying, they can <u>jam networks</u> and <u>choke up mailboxes</u>.

Cookies and spam are annoying — especially if you're on a diet...

Hmmm, there are some very <u>naughty</u> people around, and the <u>Internet</u>'s a useful tool for them. Some of the things I've talked about on this page are annoying (like <u>spam</u>), some are quite serious (like <u>fraud</u>), and some of it's <u>dangerous</u>. You've got to be <u>sensible</u> when you use the Internet.

Section 3.2 — Revision Summary

Bit of a wordy section that one. Lots to take in, so as usual I've done you a little list of questions. These will help you check whether you've really been reading these pages, or just looking at them while your brain is wondering what you're going to give it for dinner. You'd be surprised how often it turns out to have been wondering about dinner...

1) Give three jobs that have been replaced by computers.

2) Give three jobs that have been created by computers.

3) What is meant by teleworking?

4) Give one advantage and one disadvantage for an employer of their staff teleworking.

5) Give three possible advantages and three possible disadvantages for an employee of teleworking.

6) What is hot-desking? Why might organisations use it?

7) Explain how ICT technology like laptops and mobile phones can help make staff more productive.

8) Suggest why having laptops and mobile phones for work doesn't always benefit staff.

9) What does ECDL stand for?

10) What is in-house training?

11) Where might you go to receive off-the-job training?

12) Give three ways that ICT can be used by companies to help them keep staff up to date.

13) When was the Data Protection Act introduced? When was it updated, and why?

14) Who does the Data Protection Act give rights to?

15) Name three things that the Computer Misuse Act of 1990 made illegal.

16) Name the Act that made it illegal to use images from the Internet without the copyright owner's permission.

17) Which Act, passed in 1974, was designed to ensure that people were as safe as possible at work?

18) Who do the Health and Safety Regulations (1992) protect?

19) What five main things should employers do, according to these Regulations?

20) What does ICOP stand for? Give three things that an ICOP might suggest.

21) How are credit card details protected when they are put onto the Internet?

22) Outline two common web scams.

23) Why might a company want to put a 'cookie' onto your computer?

24) Explain why chatrooms can be dangerous.

25) Explain what the following computer problems are: a) Viruses   b) Spam.

Using the Internet

When you think about it, the <u>Internet</u> has had a pretty big impact on people's lives. You can now use it to <u>work</u>, to <u>shop</u>, to listen to <u>music</u>, to <u>chat</u> to your mates... just about everything important.

There's More to the Internet Than Just Web Browsing

Here's some examples of what people use the Internet for...
Most of these things are covered in more detail elsewhere in this book.

1) <u>E-mail</u> — this is the biggest use of all. It's completely changed the way people <u>communicate</u>. It means you can easily stay in contact with people <u>all over the world</u>. And because it's so huge, it's already covered on both <u>page 31</u> and <u>page 75</u> of this book. Have a look.

2) <u>Downloading music</u> — this is changing the way record companies <u>publish</u> music. Rather than buying CDs, many people now simply download the songs they want from the Internet. See <u>page 87</u> for more. Some <u>radio stations</u> also use <u>streaming</u> to broadcast on the Internet.

<u>Streaming media</u> — this is when music or videos are <u>broadcast live</u> on the Internet. Using tiny webcams, it's easy to broadcast from remote locations. This means you can watch exciting events <u>live</u>, like someone scaling Everest.

3) Getting the latest <u>news</u> — whether it's political news, celebrity news, or football news, it's all out there on the <u>web</u>. And unlike TV news programmes or printed news, you can <u>search</u> for the particular thing you want to find out about. Plus, it's always <u>up-to-date</u>.

4) <u>Online shopping</u> and <u>auctions</u> — very handy, but also potentially dodgy if you're not careful. This is covered on <u>page 68</u>.

5) <u>Online banking</u> — this is becoming more and more popular, as people's busy lives mean they can't always make it to their local branch during opening hours. Find out more on <u>page 70</u>.

You no longer have to leave the house.
But you still should.

6) <u>Booking holidays</u> — the Internet is swarming with <u>travel websites</u> and last minute holiday offers. You can use it to <u>research</u> your holiday and book your flights and hotel. It's often <u>cheaper</u> too. Have a look at <u>page 69</u> for more details.

7) <u>Paying bills</u> — many companies now allow you to pay your bills over the Internet. It's often more convenient for the company as well as the customer, so some even offer a <u>discount</u>. See <u>page 70</u>.

8) <u>Chat rooms</u> — these are special websites that people visit to have <u>virtual conversations</u> with other users. They allow people to 'chat' to others with similar interests at any time and without leaving home, but there are <u>safety concerns</u> about chat rooms. See <u>page 80</u>.

9) <u>Discussion forums</u> — these are covered on <u>page 83</u>.

I've got a problem at work...

Tell us about it.

Ook eek chatter.

What?

Using the Internet

Here's some info about a couple of Internet uses we <u>haven't</u> covered yet. I can see you're <u>excited</u>...

The Internet is Great if You Have Unusual Interests

One of the best things about the Internet is that millions of people use it. If you have an <u>unusual hobby</u>, then you can easily find others on the web to chat to or who can give you <u>advice</u>.

> Some <u>small specialist shops</u> and specialist Internet <u>radio stations</u> only exist because they can reach people all over the world through the Internet. For example, <u>www.mailorder-beads.co.uk</u> is a specialist bead shop. The owners use the Internet a lot to buy and sell their goods. Most of their business comes through the Internet so without it, the shop would probably not exist. So the Internet is good for the owners and good for people who, erm, like buying beads.

You can Discuss things on Online Forums

<u>Forums</u> let people post messages about a topic. Then you can read what other people have written and add your own message if you want to. This builds up into an <u>online conversation</u>. Unlike <u>chat rooms</u>, messages wait for replies and are kept for a very long time. People from all over the world can take part.

> Some forums are run by organisations and these are <u>moderated</u>. 'Moderated' means that messages are <u>checked</u> to make sure they're suitable before the public sees them. Some forums are private and only <u>members</u> can use them. These might <u>not</u> be moderated.
>
> There are forums on almost <u>anything</u> — including pet rats, engineering and <u>lots</u> on Star Trek. Some are obviously just for fun (or whatever Star Trek is) but lots of them are really <u>useful</u> to people — e.g. those dedicated to certain <u>jobs</u> allow people to share problems and ideas. <u>Pressure groups</u> also use them to promote awareness about particular issues.
>
> See for yourself at <u>http://groups.google.com</u> (note — no www this time).

But don't forget the Downsides

The Internet does many cool things, but it's not <u>all</u> good...

1) Almost <u>anyone</u> can add to the Internet so there's <u>unpleasant</u> and <u>unreliable</u> stuff out there. It's <u>really hard</u> to stop this Internet abuse, especially if it comes from <u>another country</u>.

2) The Internet provides <u>criminals</u> with lots of opportunities for scams and fraud.

3) Look back at page 80 for more detail on these and other problems.

There's unpleasant stuff out there.

The Internet — bringing odd people together...

No matter how <u>strange</u> your hobby is (lentil-flicking, upside-down darts, octopus racing) there will be others on the <u>Internet</u> who share your passion. Which is a good thing. Probably. But before you go joyfully in search of fellow lentil flickers, take a minute to absorb those <u>downsides</u> too.

Mobile Phones

Mobiles first went <u>mainstream</u> in the early eighties, but in those days it was just American yuppies in suits speaking into something the size of a radio and thinking they looked <u>cool</u>. How times have changed — they're now the size of a <u>postage stamp</u>, and just <u>look</u> at what you can do with them...

Mobiles Are Very Convenient

In addition to helping you annoy people on the train, mobiles have the following <u>benefits</u>:

1) You can get through to the person you want <u>wherever they are</u>. This is especially handy for people who <u>travel</u> for their job (and, of course, for jealous girlfriends).

2) Some people feel <u>safer</u> if they have a mobile, because if they get into trouble they can phone for help. Some drivers and hill-walkers take mobiles out with them for that reason.

3) The mobile phone networks 'know' where a phone is. This means that police can <u>trace</u> a criminal using their mobile phone. With the <u>owner's permission</u>, this information can be used by <u>other</u> people too — so bosses could trace their employees, or parents could trace their children.

Mobiles Are Used for Communicating in Other Ways Too

1) You can use <u>text messages</u> to contact someone without disturbing them or others. It's more <u>expensive</u> to have a text conversation than a normal voice one though.

2) Lots of phones can display <u>WAP (Wireless Application Protocol)</u> pages. These are like very simple <u>web pages</u>. Titchy screens make them difficult to use, but WAP can be really useful if you're travelling. You can even get <u>e-mail</u> by WAP. <u>Laterooms.com</u> sells hotel rooms by WAP.

3) There are lots of <u>local information WAP sites</u> that'll tell you where the nearest restaurants, cash points and so on are. This works because your mobile network 'knows' which post-code area the phone is in. Clever stuff, and very handy when you're in a strange place.

4) <u>Camera phones</u> are more expensive, but can send still or video pictures. Some estate agents use them, and they're good for keeping in touch with people you don't see very often. You can even watch the football highlights on them...

5) If you've got a laptop computer, some mobile phones let you connect to the <u>Internet</u> while you're on the move. Great for hard-working commuters and bored travellers alike.

Mobiles Do Have Their Drawbacks Though...

Surprise surprise — it's not all good news. Seems to be a constant theme in ICT.

1) Mobiles seem <u>out-of-date</u> really quickly and people replace them unnecessarily. This is expensive, and they <u>can't be recycled</u> easily.

2) Mobile calls are generally more <u>expensive</u> than fixed line calls.

3) People are worried that the radio signals from mobiles might <u>damage health</u>.

4) The phone networks need <u>transmitter stations</u>. These are <u>ugly</u> and give out more powerful radio signals than the phones do, which might be <u>harmful</u> to the health of people who live nearby.

5) Not everywhere is in the range of a <u>mobile network</u>. They don't work in very remote areas or in some buildings. This isn't very helpful if there's an emergency in an out-of-range area.

6) Some mobile users don't consider other people. It can be <u>annoying</u> when a phone rings somewhere like the cinema or theatre.

Digital Broadcasting

Digital broadcasting is replacing the older method called analogue broadcasting. Digital broadcasts are better quality — they're never 'fuzzy' because they don't usually get interference. Information can be sent too, e.g. digital radios can display the name of the song being played.

Some Broadcasts Reach Lots of People at the Same Time

1) Digital TV and radio stations are transmitted as radio waves, like the older analogue system.

2) You need digital receivers to decode the signal and turn it into sound and, for TV, pictures.

3) Receivers can be set-top boxes or they can be integrated into a TV, radio or home computer.

4) You also need a good aerial or a satellite dish.

5) Each channel broadcasts programmes at fixed times during the day.

Some Programmes are Available on Demand

1) If you're listening to music through the Internet, you can choose the programme you want to listen to — it'll be played through the Internet just for you and just when you want it.

See for yourself at www.bbc.co.uk/radio

2) You can do this with video too, but you need a much faster Internet connection.

3) That's the main problem with broadcasting on demand at the moment — you need a fast connection to get even reasonably good quality sound and pictures. But in the future, fast enough connections will probably become the norm. This could revolutionise the way we watch and listen. Why would you wait for a programme to come on if you could just choose it online and enjoy it straight away?

Digital Broadcasts Use Data Compression and Encryption

1) TV or radio programmes are stored as files on computer. Before a programme is broadcast, the data is compressed to make it take up less space. This makes it quicker to transmit.

2) Compression works by missing out bits of detail in the sound and picture that we don't usually notice. This limits the quality but is still better than the analogue alternative, which suffers from interference.

3) Sometimes TV programmes are encrypted with a secret code. To decode it, you need to buy a decoder key card. This makes pay per view and subscription channels possible.

A digital TV set top box with slots for decoder key cards

You Get loads More Choice With Digital Broadcasting

1) You can fit loads of digital TV and radio channels in the airwave space of one older analogue channel. That's why there can be loads of different digital channels.

2) This means broadcasters are able to make specialist radio channels for the sort of music you like.

3) Subscription and pay per view TV mean that you only pay for channels with the sort of stuff on that you like to watch.

Amazing — we've even made digital telly sound boring...

I remember the good old days when you had BBC1, BBC2, ITV and that was it. These days there's more channels than there's Smarties in a really big tube of... well, Smarties. But is choice really such a good thing, e.g. is it actually a good thing that you can watch Friends 24 hours a day... Hmmm.

ICT for Entertainment and Leisure

Computers were originally invented for doing really <u>serious</u> tasks like decoding <u>enemy messages</u> and flying <u>space rockets</u>. It didn't take long, though, for people to find much more <u>entertaining</u> uses for them.

Computer Games Keep Getting More Sophisticated

1) The basic idea behind computer games hasn't really changed, but they've become much more <u>realistic</u>. A driving game on a new console will have high quality <u>graphics</u> and realistic <u>sound</u>. Some games even let you feel a <u>vibration</u> when you crash.

1983   *2003*

2) The main reason games are getting better is that computers are getting more <u>powerful</u>. Faster processing means that the console can draw much more <u>detail</u> on the screen.

3) <u>Feedback controllers</u> and <u>digitally recorded sound</u> also help to make games more realistic.

4) Most new consoles let you play games with other people via the <u>Internet</u>.

5) The most sophisticated type of games are <u>virtual reality</u> games. <u>Sensors</u> are attached to the player and tell the computer how the player is moving. The player sees a virtual world through a headset with tiny screens. This needs <u>lots</u> of computing power and the hardware's very <u>expensive</u>. That's why you only see them in games centres.

Digital Recordings are Better Now Too

Digital recordings of video and sound (CDs, DVDs, Minidisks) have almost completely <u>replaced</u> older analogue recordings (tapes). When stuff is recorded digitally it's stored on disc as <u>digital code</u>.

1) The <u>quality</u> of digital recordings like DVDs and CDs is much better, because the digital code can be 'read' from the disc <u>more reliably</u>. Discs are also more <u>practical</u> because you can skip to the bit you want rather than having to wind through a tape.

Video editing.

2) Now that we have hard drive video recorders and DVD recorders, videotape will end up being completely <u>replaced</u> — just like audio tapes are being replaced with CDs.

3) <u>Digital cameras</u> have many advantages over "normal film" cameras — you only print the photos you like, you can edit them on the computer and you can even take short videos with them. As a result, old-style cameras might soon be a thing for museums.

4) <u>Digital camcorders</u> have replaced the old analogue ones in the same way — the videos are better quality, the cameras are smaller and you can use software to edit them on the computer and get them just the way you want them.

5) Digital music can be <u>compressed</u> by taking out some of the sounds we don't really notice. This makes it take up less room. That's why <u>minidisks</u> are so small.

ICT for Entertainment and Leisure

You Can Download Music and Video

If you have an Internet connection, you can <u>download</u> stuff.
You really need a <u>broadband</u> connection or lots of <u>patience</u>.
Downloading takes <u>much longer</u> than web browsing.

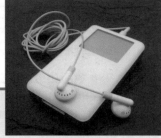
An iPod

1) Lots of record labels let you <u>legally</u> download music for a price. You pay <u>less</u> than you'd pay for a CD and you can choose just the tracks that <u>you</u> want. Good stuff.

2) To make sound files smaller and quicker to download, they're saved as a <u>compressed format</u> like <u>MP3</u>. The sound quality's not quite as good as a CD, but the files are much <u>smaller</u>.

3) It's easy to <u>copy</u> downloaded music onto small <u>MP3 players</u> like iPods. These have no moving parts so they never skip like CD players can.

4) You can do all this with <u>video</u> too, but the files are much <u>bigger</u>. When Internet <u>connection speeds</u> get quicker, downloading video will become more popular.

Computers Are Great — So Carry One in Your Pocket...

<u>Personal Digital Assistants (PDAs)</u> are pocket computers. They're not as powerful as desktop or laptop computers and the screens are pretty small, but they can be really <u>useful</u>.

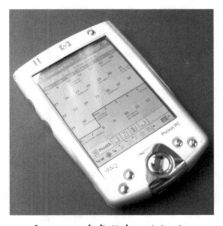
A personal digital assistant

1) You can use <u>personal organiser software</u> to keep an <u>appointments diary</u>. You can <u>synchronise</u> this with the diary on a desktop computer.

2) You can do basic <u>word processing</u> and <u>spreadsheets</u>, although entering text with the 'pen' or mini keyboard is quite fiddly.

3) Expensive PDAs link to the <u>Internet</u> through the mobile phone networks. You can then use them to <u>e-mail</u> and browse the web.

4) Most will play back digital <u>video</u>, <u>photos</u> and <u>sound</u>. Some can <u>record</u> too.

Starting on a sensible note, PDAs are good because they're so helpful to people <u>travelling on business</u>. But apart from that, they're really cool and people will buy them just so they can play <u>videos</u>, share their <u>digital photos</u> and <u>music</u> and <u>show off</u> to their mates. You watch, it'll be the same as what happened with mobiles and laptops — you start off with just rich executives using them for business purposes, and then a couple of years down the line every nine-year old has one.

Virtual realities and digital assistants — it's getting weird now...

I saw this thing about <u>virtual reality</u> on the TV. It said that in the future virtual reality technology would become <u>so sophisticated</u> that in all probability we're all living in one right now without realising it, and <u>nothing is really real</u> at all. Freaked me out at the time, but now I know it's true. I am Keanu.

ICT in the Community

ICT has now become as much a part of the community as <u>coffee mornings</u> and the local pub.

Lots of Places Provide Internet Access

There are various places where the general public can access the Internet.

1) You can use an <u>Internet café</u> to <u>surf the web</u> or <u>check e-mail</u>. These are funny-looking cafés where you can pay to use a computer. You can have a coffee while you're there too. They're really useful when you are away from home, or if you don't have a computer.

2) Most <u>public libraries</u> and many <u>post offices</u> have computers for <u>web browsing</u> too. It's often <u>free</u> for students and certain other people but you don't get coffee or cake.

3) You might also see fancy web-browsing public <u>telephones</u> with <u>touch screens</u>. These crop up in public places like shopping centres and airports.

Touch Screen Terminals are Popping up Everywhere

Information terminals with touch screens can be found everywhere now. The <u>touch screen</u> technology makes them <u>easy</u> for everybody to use, even really computer-phobic types.

- • <u>Tourist offices</u> often have them to help you find out about local tourist attractions.

- • You might also find them at <u>bus</u> or <u>train stations</u> to help you buy tickets or plan journeys.

- • <u>Job centres</u> also have touch screens to help you look for jobs that match your specifications.

A touch screen computer providing public transport information.

All Public Services Have Information on the Web

All public services have websites where you can get information. Here's some examples:

1) If you want to know about the local area — places of interest, history, things to do, accommodation — look at the local <u>tourist office</u>'s website.

2) If you're interested in <u>local politics</u>, look at your local government's website. You'll be able to read about important local issues and policies. These websites often host <u>online discussions</u> giving you the chance to voice opinions and ask questions.

3) If you want quick advice without visiting the doctor, <u>NHS Direct</u> has a huge online information system with information about common illnesses and medical conditions (www.nhsdirect.nhs.uk). By giving people advice about non-serious problems, this frees up GPs' time to deal with <u>more serious</u> problems.

Doctor Doctor, I feel like a pair of curtains...

Those touch screen computers in public places are really <u>well-designed</u>. Not only are they hard to damage, they're really easy for <u>anybody</u> to use. Even your gran. Go and find one in your local area and play with it (in a nice way). Then you'll have a better idea of what I'm going on about.

ICT and Travel

Thanks to various clever ICT inventions, it's now easier than ever to get from A to B.

ICT Can Help You To Get Around...

TRAVEL INFORMATION AND BOOKINGS

1) For public transport information, just go on the Internet and download the most recent timetables.

2) The Internet's also an easy way to book journeys in advance, whether you're going by train, coach, boat or plane.

3) If you're in a big shopping centre or station, you can get travel info from information terminals (see previous page). Some let you book tickets too.

PLANNING JOURNEYS

1) Route planning software uses data about roads and driving speeds to work out the most efficient route for a journey. You just enter your starting point and destination. Trucking companies and travelling sales people use this a lot. It even works for complicated journeys with lots of stops.

2) Various internet sites, e.g. www.multimap.com, can also help you plan a journey. These sites are like online road atlases. You can look at (and print) maps of where you're going and zoom in and out to get the level of detail you need. As well as maps, they also provide general information on the area you're looking at, e.g. hotels and restaurants. All pretty handy stuff.

3) ICT can also get you instant traffic information in your car — Trafficnet use sensors by major roads to measure the speed of the traffic. This information is sent out to the Internet and to in-car receivers by radio. See for yourself at http://vauxhall.co.uk/trafficnet (no www).

...and it can Stop you from Getting Lost

GPS stands for Global Positioning System and is used to pinpoint your location by connecting to GPS satellites.

1) GPS is used as a navigating tool for outdoor sports like sailing and hill-walking. A GPS receiver will tell you your exact position, so it's really useful for walking in fog or when all you can see is sea.

2) It takes less skill to use GPS than it does to use a compass. But the receiver's battery powered, so if it runs out you could be in trouble. They don't work well in cities either.

3) The GPS satellites were incredibly expensive to produce and position, but luckily we don't have to pay to use them. Receivers cost between £80 (for a basic one) and £500. The simple ones show just a grid reference of where you are. Posher ones show where you are on a little map.

CAR NAVIGATION SYSTEMS

Avoid this.

If a computer knows where you are by using GPS and has access to map data, it can give you directions to where you want to go.

Navigation systems in some cars use this idea to give the driver instructions, with the help of a screen with arrows and an artificial voice.

Navigation systems can even use live traffic information from special transmitters to guide you around traffic jams. Very clever stuff.

It's only a matter of time before the cars drive themselves...

Car navigation systems, instant traffic jam information, well I don't know... Sometimes I think ICT technology goes too far. Sure, it's clever, but do we really need a computer to tell us which way to turn... Personally, I prefer to live on the edge and take my chances following the road signs.

ICT for People with Particular Needs

People with <u>disabilities</u> might need variations on the standard equipment to use computers, but once they have these, ICT can be <u>really helpful</u> to them.

Some Equipment Helps People With Sensory Impairments

ICT for the Blind or Partially Sighted

Computer systems can be adapted to make them easier for people to use...

1) For people with <u>partial</u> sight, changing <u>screen settings</u> can help. You can change the <u>colour scheme</u>, screen <u>resolution</u> and font sizes to make it clearer. You can also use special keyboards with large coloured keys that are easier to see.

2) For blind people, special hardware is available — <u>braille keyboards</u> make it easy to <u>type</u>, and documents can be <u>printed</u> in braille with special printers.

3) <u>Screen readers</u> are pieces of software that use <u>speech synthesis</u> technology to <u>read out</u> and <u>describe</u> what's on the screen. On compatible web pages, they'll even describe images for you.

> Watching TV is easier now too — **digital TV** can be set up to receive **audio descriptions** of the action on the programme. This helps partially sighted or blind people to understand what's going on.

ICT for People With Hearing Difficulties

1) People with hearing difficulties can still use most computer functions normally. One thing you can do though is set up the computer to <u>display visual icons</u> rather than using <u>sound cues</u>.

2) <u>DVDs</u> are much better than videotapes as you can turn <u>subtitles</u> on.

3) Many recent communication technologies like <u>e-mail</u> and <u>texting</u> work really well for people with hearing problems. Being able to set mobile phones to <u>vibrate</u> or <u>flash</u> is also very useful.

4) <u>Video conferencing</u> can be used to hold a conversations by <u>sign language</u> or <u>lip reading</u>.

5) <u>Textphones</u> are an older system that replace a standard telephone with a <u>keyboard</u> and a <u>screen</u>. What you type appears on both screens — a bit like a chat-room. Both sender and receiver need a <u>textphone machine</u>.

6) Telephones and public venues can be fitted with <u>induction loops</u>. These are a bit like <u>transmitters</u> that send sound directly into a hearing aid. Telephones can also have special amplifiers fitted to make them much louder.

> There are also technologies available for people with **multiple disabilities**, e.g. for people who can't see **or** hear, you can get feelable 'screens' which show braille. This helps them to communicate.

ICT is Useful for People With Language Difficulties

If you have to communicate in a <u>language</u> you're not used to, you're likely to have difficulties.

1) <u>Dictionary software</u> can help you to quickly <u>translate</u> individual words.

2) <u>Learning software</u> can help you to practice an unfamiliar language with exercises where you can <u>hear</u> phrases spoken. It can also <u>record</u> your voice and play it back so you can see how well you've done.

3) Most word processing packages can check your <u>spelling</u> in different languages and check that your sentences <u>make sense</u>.

ICT for People with Particular Needs

Some Systems Help People With Physical Disabilities

ICT technologies can help people with all kinds of physical disabilities to live normal lives.

Computer systems can be adapted

a trackerball

1) Many people find mice difficult to use — there are many alternatives available such as trackerballs, joysticks and touch pads. People with limited hand movement can get specially designed keyboards that are less fiddly to use.

2) Voice recognition software can be used by people with little or no hand movement. It lets you speak to the computer to navigate menus and dictate writing.

3) Even if you are severely limited, you can still control a computer with switches carefully arranged — Stephen Hawking is a famous example of someone who uses ICT in this way.

ICT can help people to become more independent

1) If you find it difficult to use ordinary shops for some reason, then you can shop on the Internet. Supermarket online services keep a list of your usual shopping. This saves all of us time, but can be especially useful if you've got a disability.

2) Teleworking (see page 76) is great if you find it hard to travel.

3) For people with limited mobility, environmental control systems can be set up to automatically close curtains, turn lights on and off, operate heaters and so on.

Computers Can Help People With Learning Difficulties

Here's some examples of the options available:

1) Multimedia software helps people who find it hard to concentrate. It uses different forms of media, e.g. pictures, sound clips and videos to keep the user interested.

2) Specialised educational software — there's a huge range of software available to help people struggling with particular things like reading or basic maths.

3) Touch screens are useful for people who struggle to use a keyboard and mouse.

4) Spell checkers can help people with dyslexia because you can set them up to check and correct your words as you type.

5) Other software can help adults with moderate learning difficulties. Software can help people develop skills for living on their own by providing real-life simulation 'games'.

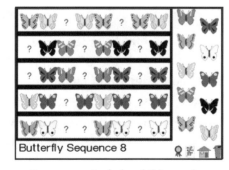
Butterfly Sequence 8

A program to help children who struggle with basic maths.

See — it's not all games and gadgets...

ICT affects everyone's daily lives a lot — in places like the UK anyway. And we're so used to it that we hardly notice it any more, it's like oxygen or something. But for some people, it can still directly and dramatically improve their life. See for yourself at www.dlf.org.uk or www.abilitynet.org.uk.

ICT for Education and Lifelong Learning

Obviously you use ICT for this Applied ICT GCSE you're doing. But it doesn't end there.
ICT can be used to help people learn about all kinds of subjects at all kinds of different stages.

ICT is Used in Schools to Create Electronic Classrooms

① COMPUTER-AIDED LEARNING (CAL) (also called e-learning) — uses software to generate on-screen learning materials. CAL software is often interactive, e.g. it might provide questions to be answered on screen, which the software will then mark for you. The software might give you hints on the topics you struggled with and even set extra questions on them.

The main potential benefit is an improvement in the quality of pupils' learning, and hopefully an increase in motivation.

The basic problem is the cost of the technology.

② INTERACTIVE WHITE BOARDS — they're like big computer screens that the whole class can see. They're interactive — you can control the computer by moving and clicking with a special pen on the board.

③ INTERNET — teachers can use the Internet to download syllabuses and teaching materials, etc. E-mail can be used to exchange ideas with other schools. The Internet's also a very handy tool for finding information on a particular topic...

Using ICT For Research

1) The Internet can be fantastic for finding out information that's completely up to date. Search engines are easy to use and with a few goes, you should be able to find exactly what you want. But you do have to be careful to make sure that information you find on the Internet is reliable.

2) Multimedia encyclopaedias are another very useful research tool. They're easier to search and the multimedia elements like audio and video clips make the stuff easier to understand and a lot more interesting.

3) Online encyclopaedias like www.britannica.com are reliable and up to date, but it does cost to subscribe to these.

ICT helps People Study from Home

Learning doesn't stop once you leave school or college — most adults will want to learn new skills at some point in their lives. One option is to do an evening class at a local college. But this isn't always convenient. If not, good old ICT can provide more options...

1) You can buy CD-ROMs and DVDs to teach you new skills, e.g. to teach you a new language or help you prepare for your driving theory test.

2) If you want to do something that's not available at your local college, you could do an online course over the Internet.

Kevin wasn't pleased with the mark he got for his online test

3) Online courses are good because you can work from home and do them when you want. But they do have drawbacks — you don't get the buzz of working together in a group and you don't have a "real" tutor teaching you who can fire questions at you.

4) However, most online courses do have chat rooms or discussion forums where you can discuss topics with other students doing the course and post questions to the course tutors.

Don't bother listening to ME — I'm just pictures and text...

This page is giving me an inferiority complex. My book can't show you animations or play you music. You can't use it to hold a video conference either. But you can use it to pass your GCSE, so there. And CGP's got a website too you know — it's at www.cgpbooks.co.uk. Have a look.

Section 3.3 — Revision Summary

Before you start doing your Unit 3 assignments, you really need to know your stuff. By now you should be an expert on how ICT has made changes to society, and I'm sure you are. But just to make sure... try these questions. Oh go on, it won't take long and it'll hurt my feelings if you don't.

1) Name six different things you can do on the Internet.

2) What is streaming media used to do?

3) Why is the Internet good for people with 'unusual interests'?

4) How do online discussion forums work?

5) Give three downsides of the Internet.

6) Explain how a mobile phone could provide evidence against a criminal.

7) Apart from sound, name three things that a mobile phone can send.

8) What does WAP stand for? What is it?

9) Give one advantage of digital broadcasting over the older analogue broadcasting method.

10) Digital data can be compressed. How is this done?

11) Why might you need a decoder key card with your digital TV box?

12) How do virtual reality games work?

13) Give two advantages of DVDs over videotapes.

14) What is MP3?

15) What is a PDA? Name three things it will do for you.

16) Name three public places where you can access the Internet.

17) How do touch screens work?
Give one example of where they might be used by the general public.

18) What kind of information does the NHS Direct website contain?

19) Give two ways that the Internet can help you plan a journey.

20) How could ICT help you to avoid getting stuck in a traffic jam?

21) What is GPS? How can it be of use to sailors?

22) It can be dangerous for mountaineers to rely on GPS — they still take a compass.
Why is it dangerous to rely on GPS?

23) Give two ways that a computer system can be adapted for a partially sighted or blind person.

24) Give two examples of how ICT can help people who are deaf or who have hearing difficulties.

25) How can ICT be used to help people learn a new language?

26) Suggest two ways that computer systems can be adapted for people with motor impairment.

27) Give three ways that ICT can help people with learning difficulties.

28) What is CAL?

29) Give two ways that adults can use ICT to learn from home.

Unit 1 Assessment Advice (Edexcel)

You have to do an <u>exam</u> for Unit 1, but <u>don't panic</u> — it's a <u>practical</u> exam on the computer, not a written paper. Just follow the instructions <u>carefully</u> and you'll be fine.

The exam is <u>2 ½ hours</u> long and offers up to <u>100 marks</u>. It will have about four <u>tasks</u>, each split into several <u>smaller tasks</u>. You'll be asked to use <u>spreadsheet</u>, <u>database</u>, <u>word-processing</u> and <u>presentation</u> software.

Don't panic.

The stuff you're meant to be able to do with each kind of software is listed below. You need to make sure you can comfortably do <u>all these things</u>...

Exam Software 1 — Spreadsheets

WHAT YOU NEED TO DO:

1) <u>Enter</u> text and numbers, and <u>format</u> the cells to match what you've entered.

2) <u>Cut</u>, <u>copy</u> and <u>paste</u> data, and <u>insert</u> and <u>delete</u> rows and columns.

3) Use <u>formulas</u>, simple <u>functions</u> and relative and absolute <u>cell references</u>.

4) Produce <u>charts</u> and <u>print</u> selected areas of the spreadsheet.

HOW TO GET THE BEST MARKS:

1) <u>Check</u> and double-check you've done what was asked, and that your spelling's right. It's really easy to make small <u>mistakes</u>, especially in formulas, that mess up the whole thing.

2) Don't waste time <u>printing</u> during the exam — you'll get time for this later.

3) If you have to produce a <u>chart</u>, make sure it has an appropriate <u>title</u> and <u>legend</u>.

4) Make sure your spreadsheet meets the <u>needs</u> of the user, and is <u>appropriate</u> in terms of presentation, layout and tone.

Exam Software 2 — Word Processing

WHAT YOU NEED TO DO:

1) <u>Enter</u>, <u>cut</u>, <u>paste</u>, <u>move</u> and <u>format</u> text.

2) Use special <u>formatting features</u> like headers, footers and bullet points.

3) Add <u>graphics</u> and <u>tables</u> to your document, and <u>word wrap</u> text around them.

4) Use <u>mail-merge</u> facilities.

HOW TO GET THE BEST MARKS:

1) Word processing is the job where you're most likely to make <u>spelling mistakes</u>, so make sure you not only <u>check</u> over your work, but also do a <u>spell-check</u>.

2) Make sure your document meets the <u>needs</u> of the user, and is <u>appropriate</u> in terms of writing style, tone, presentation and layout.

3) Don't bother <u>printing</u> during the exam — you'll get time for this later.

4) Make sure you know about the general <u>layout</u> of letters, memos, faxes etc.

Unit 1 Assessment Advice (Edexcel)

Exam Software 3 — Databases

WHAT YOU NEED TO DO:

1) Prepare the database structure and validation rules for different data types (e.g. text, date).

2) Enter data using data entry forms.

3) Make a relationship between fields in two tables.

4) Do searches and sorts and produce reports to show the results.

HOW TO GET THE BEST MARKS:

1) Before the exam look at lots of examples of databases and database reports in order to learn about how they should look and be organised.

2) Databases have some tricky bits like creating validation rules and using related tables. Make sure you get plenty of practice until you are comfortable with all these bits.

3) Double-check your work for errors.

Exam Software 4 — Presentation Software

WHAT YOU NEED TO DO:

1) Decide on a structure and navigation route through the presentation.

2) Create or find the separate components of the presentation — text, images, sound, videos.

3) Produce frames, layers, backgrounds and eventually entire slides.

4) Combine the components to create a final presentation, and edit it where necessary.

HOW TO GET THE BEST MARKS:

1) Look at a variety of presentations designed for different purposes, and learn which layouts work best for which audiences and which purposes.

2) Pay careful attention to your writing style, tone, clarity and consistency.

3) Make sure your presentation gets across the message it's supposed to.

4) Double-check your work for errors which could lose you vital marks.

Pre-release Materials from Edexcel will help you to Prepare

1) Pre-release materials for the exam will be released each year in October.

2) These will tell you the scenario for the exam, e.g. it might be a fictional organisation that all the tasks will be based around. They'll also contain various activities to help you prepare.

3) It's really important that you study all these materials and do all the activities in them.

4) As well as this, you should also make sure you can do everything in the past papers from the last couple of years. If you can do all that you'll be absolutely fine, I promise.

Lucky old you — a lovely exam. Mmmmm...

Some final advice... make sure you know how to print from all the packages onto single A4 sheets (the exams are big on that), remember to save your work regularly and read all instructions carefully.

Unit 2 Assessment Advice (Edexcel)

Unit Two is assessed by a written <u>portfolio</u>. It is split into two main parts:
— Describing and evaluating the systems in a <u>real organisation</u> (tasks a and b)
— Planning, designing and implementing a system <u>of your own</u> (tasks c and d)

Task a — Report on the Purposes for Which an Organisation Uses ICT

WHAT YOU NEED TO DO:

1) Choose an organisation (or a department of a large organisation) to study.
   Then <u>visit</u> it to look around and interview people — have a list of questions
   with you and take careful notes of the answers. Include these in your portfolio.

WORTH UP TO 10 MARKS

2) Give a <u>clear description</u> of the work of the organisation. You need to cover its main functions
   and other relevant information, like the number of people who work there.

3) Identify systems they use and their <u>objectives</u> (what's <u>supposed to happen</u> if it works).
   Don't talk about how well it achieves these objectives. You'll be doing that in task b.

HOW TO GET THE BEST MARKS:

1) You need to show you understand the <u>wide range</u> of ICT uses. It might not be possible to
   cover all of them and if it's a very large organisation, you can write about just one
   department, e.g. sales or finance. But make sure you <u>do</u> cover a good range of uses.

2) Don't just list the uses — you need to <u>fully explain</u> the <u>purposes</u> of using ICT for the range of
   ICT systems you find. For example you may say that a video store uses a database showing
   who has borrowed each film, and when it is due back. But you should go on to explain why —

   > "the video store needs to know if a film is overdue so it can apply fines. It also needs to be
   > able to tell people who want to hire a particular film when it will be available."

Task b — Report on an ICT System and How it Meets the Organisation's Needs

WHAT YOU NEED TO DO:

WORTH UP TO 14 MARKS

1) Describe the <u>hardware</u> and <u>software</u> used in one of the ICT systems from Task 1.

2) You need to describe at least <u>one</u> piece of hardware from <u>each</u> of the following five groups:
   - <u>input</u> devices
   - <u>storage</u> devices
   - <u>processing</u> devices
   - <u>output</u> devices
   - <u>ports</u> and <u>cables</u>

HOW TO GET THE BEST MARKS:

1) Include <u>specific detail</u> in your descriptions — like specifications, speeds, amount of memory
   and storage space, etc. Make sure you cover all five types or you are throwing marks away.

2) Don't just list the items, go on to <u>evaluate</u> them. Evaluating involves the following:
   - Saying whether the <u>objectives/needs</u> have been met.
   - Saying what it <u>can</u> do, compared to what the business <u>needs</u> it to do.
   - <u>Suggesting alternatives</u> that would meet the needs better.

3) Remember that the different parts of the system don't just work on their own.
   So explain how the different components in the system are <u>connected</u>.

Unit 2 Assessment Advice (Edexcel)

The <u>second part</u> of Unit 2 is about creating your <u>own ICT system</u>.

Task c — Produce a Design Specification for a New ICT System

WORTH UP TO 17 MARKS

WHAT YOU NEED TO DO:

1) The first thing is to <u>identify the problem</u> you're going to solve.
   It <u>doesn't</u> need to be for the organisation from the earlier tasks,
   but it can be if they've got a good problem you think you can tackle.

2) Once you've got the problem, you can begin to <u>plan the project</u>. Ask yourself:

   - What are the <u>objectives</u> for the system?
   - What <u>data</u> will I need to collect?
   - What are the <u>tasks</u> that need to be done?
   - Which <u>software</u> am I going to use and why?
   - What will the <u>user</u> need to do?
   - How much <u>time</u> do I have?
   - What <u>data types</u> will be used?
   - What <u>order</u> should the tasks go in?
   - What <u>hardware</u> will I need?
   - Can I solve this problem at all?

3) Produce a <u>design specification</u>. This should be a detailed description of the design for the ICT
   system. You must specify <u>input</u>, <u>process</u> and <u>output</u> requirements, <u>information sources</u>,
   and the type of <u>application software</u> needed. You should include:

   - A <u>data flow diagram</u> (see p63) to give an overview of your
     new system and show how the information will flow through it.
   - Some <u>rough designs</u> for input forms which will be used.
   - <u>Initial designs</u> for what the output will look like.
   - Final designs with <u>full details</u> of how the system will look and work.

4) Don't forget a detailed <u>test plan</u> in your report — this explains how you plan to test your
   system, surprisingly. Think of the objectives you've set for your system and build it around
   those. You should also say:

   - How many tests you are going to do.
   - Which data you are going to use.
   - What results you expect.

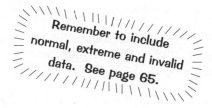
Remember to include normal, extreme and invalid data. See page 65.

HOW TO GET THE BEST MARKS:

1) Make sure you choose a problem that requires a <u>complex solution</u>.
   Examples of this are a relational database or a spreadsheet that has linked sheets.

2) If possible it's a good idea to produce an initial design and get feedback on it from your
   users. Then include this feedback in your design specification.

3) Include in your design specification a description of the '<u>success factors</u>' of your system —
   i.e. what each part of your system is supposed to do. This will help you to evaluate at the
   end how well your system does what it's supposed to.

4) The best design specifications will make it possible for <u>anyone with IT knowledge</u> to pick up
   your design and implement the system.

5) The test plan should effectively test <u>everything</u> your system can do.

But <u>you're not finished yet</u> — turn over the page for the last task of Unit 2...

Unit 2 Assessment Advice (Edexcel)

Task d — Implement, Test and Evaluate the System

WORTH UP TO 17 MARKS

WHAT YOU NEED TO DO:

1) Next you'll have to actually <u>make</u> the system.
You'll have to show <u>evidence</u> of the system being developed and used.

2) Record <u>how</u> you made it, any <u>problems</u> you had along the way and how you solved them.

3) Produce a <u>user guide</u> to show other people how to use your system. You could do this as a booklet or as online help. You might use <u>screen images</u> to help you explain how to do the various tasks.

4) <u>Test</u> your system. Use a range of data and test against <u>all</u> likely initial conditions.

5) Record all your tests <u>clearly</u>, for example in a table.

6) Use the results of your tests to <u>evaluate</u> your system — say how well it did its intended job. Comment on its <u>efficiency</u> and how <u>robust</u> it is (if it crashes or goes wrong a lot, it's not very robust). Provide evidence of any <u>improvements</u> you made following testing and explain them.

HOW TO GET THE BEST MARKS:

1) The best way to show <u>evidence</u> of the system being made is to keep a <u>development diary</u>. This is basically a written <u>commentary</u> of what you did. It should include lots of screen-shots and <u>describe and explain</u> what's going on in each one. See page 65 for more details.

2) For high marks your evaluation should be really detailed and include evidence of evaluation by a <u>third party</u>. So basically you get someone else to try out your system and find out what they thought.

3) From this evaluation it's also a good idea to recommend a few <u>improvements</u> for the future.

4) Evaluate your <u>user documentation</u>. Again, get <u>someone else</u> to try using it and give you feedback.

5) For the best marks your user documentation should make it possible for <u>anyone</u> to use your system — they shouldn't need to be experts with systems like yours.

Tony's system was designed so anyone could use it. The input screen looked a lot like a simple computer game.

Maybe an Exam would have been easier...

Hmmm, this 'no exam' lark might not be all it's cracked up to be. Seems like a lot of work. But on the other hand, if you put a bit of <u>effort</u> in, you've got all the time you need to <u>make sure</u> you end up with something really good, that'll get you <u>top marks</u>. So it's all worth it. Happy ending.

Unit 3 Assessment Advice (Edexcel)

Your unit 3 work takes the form of a portfolio evaluating how ICT affects everyday life.
It's broken down into five tasks. You have to evaluate uses of ICT (tasks a to d), and ICT laws (task e).

Task a — Write a report about the Impact of ICT on Your Own Activities

WORTH UP TO 11 MARKS

WHAT YOU NEED TO DO:

1) Task a is all about evaluating your own use of ICT — at home and at school or college.

2) You can choose any types of ICT technology that you use. Below are some examples:

- Examples of personal ICT use — Games console, Internet (e.g. buying on ebay), laptop.
- Examples of social ICT use — Mobile phone, e-mail, Internet (e.g. chatrooms).
- Examples of school/college work use — Internet research, spreadsheet software, word-processing.

3) For each of your ICT uses, you need to describe how they meet your needs,
e.g. Social use of ICT: a mobile phone. Explain that you need it to contact your friends and family while you're out. You could go on to describe the variety of ways in which the phone enables you to contact them, like text or photo messages, voicemail and so on.

HOW TO GET THE BEST MARKS:

1) Choose at least three examples of your use of ICT, one from each of these three categories:

i) Personal use (on your own).   ii) Social use (with others).   iii) School/college work-related use.

2) Evaluate how well ICT meets your needs — this is the thing that can really boost your marks.
E.g. Work related use of ICT: Using the Internet to do research for your History project.
Explain how and why you use it, but go on to say how well the Internet meets your needs.

3) Think about drawbacks as well as positive points — e.g. "Although the Internet allowed me easy access to a large amount of information, it is often difficult to tell whether information is reliable and un-biased."

Task b — Write a report about the Impact of ICT on an Adult in Employment

Task b is similar to a, but this time you're writing about an adult in employment.
The best way is to interview a suitable adult and get them to tell you how they use ICT.

WORTH UP TO 14 MARKS

WHAT YOU NEED TO DO:

1) You've got to cover their personal, social and work-related uses of ICT, both at home and at work.

2) You also need to include how using ICT has changed this person's working style and practices.

3) Just like in task a, describe and explain their use of ICT, then evaluate how well it meets their needs (e.g. "Using e-mail to communicate with work colleagues works well, because she can attach extra information like copies of reports. However, for complicated cases she still finds it best to meet in person, because things can be explained more clearly.")

HOW TO GET THE BEST MARKS:

1) Again the key is good evaluation, including looking at drawbacks as well as positives.

Turn over for advice on the remaining three tasks of Unit 3...

Unit 3 Assessment Advice (Edexcel)

Task c — Write a Report on the Impact of ICT on Someone with Special Needs

WORTH UP TO 11 MARKS

WHAT YOU NEED TO DO:

1) This time you're writing about someone with special or particular needs. Right at the start, you need to say what those needs are, and link the uses of ICT to those needs.

HOW TO GET THE BEST MARKS:

1) Remember, describe then evaluate (e.g. "He has voice recognition software but this does not work well for him as it still uses some onscreen prompts. Therefore he is thinking of trying a Braille keyboard.")

2) Choose your ICT uses carefully. You don't have to write about every bit of ICT they use, but you should give a good range of different uses which are representative of how they use ICT. You should explain how ICT technology meets their personal, social and work-related needs.

Task d — Write a Report on the Impact of ICT in Your Local Community

WORTH UP TO 11 MARKS

WHAT YOU NEED TO DO:

1) Task d is about your local community. First make sure you say where your local community is — sorry to state the obvious, but it's pretty important.

2) In this report you should link ICT use to the needs of the community — e.g. "The public library offers free Internet use to the unemployed. This can help people to find work, and can also help them to develop new skills."

HOW TO GET THE BEST MARKS:

1) You should cover a range of different uses that your local community makes of ICT. Aim for at least three quite different uses.

2) And as usual, make sure you evaluate as well as describe — e.g. "Free use of the Internet does benefit the unemployed, but other people have to pay to use it. This could discourage some groups, like the elderly, who might find the Internet useful for other reasons, e.g. entertainment and meeting people."

Task e — Explain the ICT Legislation Protecting People and Groups

WORTH UP TO 11 MARKS

WHAT YOU NEED TO DO:

1) Task e is about ICT legislation. It doesn't have to be a separate section in your portfolio — you could cover the relevant legislation in each of the other four sections.

2) Link the legislation to the uses you've described — pick the law that's most relevant to the person/group you've investigated. Describe the law, who it protects and why it was introduced.

HOW TO GET THE BEST MARKS:

1) Evaluate how it might affect the people in your reports.

2) Make sure you comment on how appropriate and effective the legislation is.

You may now be wishing ICT had NO effect on your life...

...perhaps even that ICT would just get lost and leave you alone. Shame on you. This portfolio may not be much fun, but at least you get to write about some fun stuff like mobiles and the Internet.

Unit 1 Assessment Advice (AQA)

The next three pages will give you lots of handy advice on your Unit 1 coursework.
There are five tasks to do which shouldn't take you more than 20 sides of A4 to cover fully.
The first three tasks are about business documents.

Task 1 — Write a Report on Documents Used By Businesses

WORTH UP TO 21 MARKS

WHAT YOU NEED TO DO:

1) Collect a range of documents produced by real businesses, e.g. leaflets, flyers, brochures. Choose at least three to review for your report.

2) Describe the documents. Make sure you write about the following:
   - Content — writing style and tone. Use of photos, diagrams, charts.
   - Layout — how the page is arranged. Columns, margins, colours, etc.
   - Purpose — What's the document for? Who's the target audience?

"We only need to review three documents?"

3) Comment on the suitability of the documents for their purpose. Explain how they try to meet the needs of their users, and comment on how well you think they've done this.

HOW TO GET THE BEST MARKS:

1) Choose documents that are quite different to each other, and that have been created using at least three different software applications (e.g. DTP, word processing, spreadsheets, databases.)

2) You must include the original documents in your portfolio. You'll lose a lot of marks if you don't. (This doesn't count towards your total of 20 sides of A4.)

3) Make sure your descriptions of the content, layout and purpose are as detailed as possible.

4) Include detailed and thoughtful evaluations of how suitable each document is for its intended users. Suggest ways that the documents could be improved based on this evaluation.

Task 2 — Produce Your Own Business Documents

WORTH UP TO 25 MARKS

WHAT YOU NEED TO DO:

1) Produce three business documents. They need to be as realistic as possible, so you could design them for a real company, or you could make up a new company which needs a set of standard documents and marketing materials. You'll need to produce several drafts of these documents before you decide on your final design (see next page).

2) Make sure your documents are fit for their purpose and audience and are well presented.

3) Use ICT tools like searches and sorts to gather and organise the information you use in the documents. Use as many different kinds of ICT tools as possible — e.g. Internet searches to find the information, spreadsheet software to turn data into charts, databases to organise and sort the data.

4) Provide evidence that you've used these ICT tools. Make screen-shots as you do your searches and sorts and paste them into a separate document. Add written explanations of what you did and why.

HOW TO GET THE BEST MARKS:

1) Each document should use two or three software applications, e.g. in a DTP advertising flyer, you could put in a chart from a spreadsheet and include edited graphics from a graphics package.

2) Your documents should demonstrate a range of writing styles and layouts. It's easier to do if you create three quite different types of document for three different purposes or audiences.

Unit 1 Assessment Advice (AQA)

Task 3 — Annotate Early Drafts and Evaluate Final Versions

WHAT YOU NEED TO DO:

1) Produce three drafts of each of your documents from Task 2. Annotate each draft to explain what corrections and improvements you're going to make in the next draft.

2) Include a written report for each document. This should explain how the features of the applications software you've used have allowed you to meet the purpose of the document.

3) Evaluate your finished documents in the report. Comment on how well you think they've met their purpose. Suggest how they could be improved further.

HOW TO GET THE BEST MARKS:

1) Don't just annotate each document with simple error corrections like spelling mistakes. Your earliest drafts should be pretty different to the finished document. At each stage your comments should show that you're evaluating your work and making real improvements in style and presentation.

2) Your annotations shouldn't just say what you're going to change in your next draft — you should give good reasons for making each of the changes. And don't make changes just for the sake of it.

3) It's fine to make a change and then decide you don't like it and change it back in a later draft. Examiners actually like that, as long as you've explained your reasoning at each stage.

4) Compare your own final documents to real commercial documents in your evaluation. Use this to say how yours could be further improved. Include any real documents you've looked at in your portfolio.

Task 4 — Write a Report on Software Used By Businesses

The fourth task is a bit different...

WHAT YOU NEED TO DO:

1) You have to write about the use by organisations of:
   - CAD/CAM software
   - sensing and control software
   - image manipulation software

2) Describe in detail the main features of each of these types of software.

3) Describe in detail why each of these types of software is used in various organisations.

HOW TO GET THE BEST MARKS:

1) Describe at least three features and reasons why it's used for each type of software.

2) Include a detailed discussion of the impact of each software type on organisations that use it.

Unit 1 Assessment Advice (AQA)

The other 19 marks available for Unit 1 come from using <u>standard ways of working</u> (see below) and from <u>verifying</u> (checking) your information sources.

Task 5 — *Show That You've Used Standard Ways of Working*

WORTH UP TO 19 MARKS

WHAT YOU NEED TO DO:

1) Use <u>standard ways of working</u> on the computer as you produce your work for this unit. This involves:
   - Using sensible <u>filenames</u> — names that would let someone else see at once what's in the file.
   - Use <u>folders</u> to organise your work — e.g. you might have a different folder for each of the five tasks in the unit. Then within each of those folders you might have folders for background information, work still in progress, finished work, etc.
   - Make <u>dated backup copies</u> of all your files and keep them in a separate folder.
   - Keep your <u>early drafts</u> and old versions of each piece of work — don't just delete them. These should have their own folder too.

2) Take <u>screen-shots</u> in Windows Explorer (or equivalent) to show how your files are organised. Paste these into a <u>separate document</u> and include a piece of writing to <u>explain</u> them.

3) Provide evidence that you've <u>verified</u> (checked) the information sources you've used in this unit. You need to include <u>references</u> to show where the information came from, and provide another source that <u>agrees</u> with it.

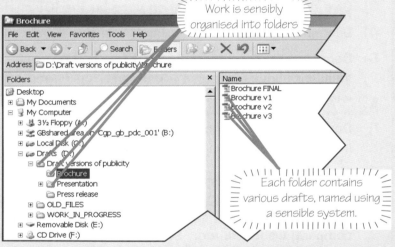

Work is sensibly organised into folders

Each folder contains various drafts, named using a sensible system.

Use screen-shots to show how you've organised your work.

HOW TO GET THE BEST MARKS:

1) Use this system <u>right from the start</u> of your portfolio work — it's much simpler than trying to fake it at the end.

2) Make sure you verify at least <u>three</u> of your information sources. If you don't verify any, the best mark you can get is 11 out of 19. It's especially important with <u>Internet sources</u>, but don't spend days verifying every single source you've used — three will do fine.

Bob really enjoyed using standard ways of working.

3) Remember that there's no single right way to organise and manage your work. The best marks are given to people who create their <u>own</u> effective directory system that suits them, and who <u>explain</u> clearly how their system works and why they've chosen to organise their work that way. Keep in mind those four points from the top of this box and after that it's up to you.

Yay, no exam! Woo-hoo! *(just a long assignment...)*

Quite a bit of work here, but nothing really tricky. I'd recommend looking back at <u>Section 1.4</u> at some point during your work for Unit 1 — it's got lots of info about business documents, standard ways of working, plus three pages on the three types of <u>software</u> you've got to report on for task 4.

Unit 2 Assessment Advice (AQA)

Unit 2 is also assessed on a written <u>portfolio</u>. It's marked out of 100, and there are four tasks which shouldn't need more than <u>20 sides of A4</u>. The <u>first two</u> are about ICT use in two organisations.

Task 1 — Report on How and Why Two Organisations Use ICT Systems

WORTH UP TO 23 MARKS

WHAT YOU NEED TO DO:

1) Choose two quite <u>different</u> organisations to study. You can find them yourself, e.g. through a family member or part-time job, but <u>check</u> with your teacher that they're OK. Then <u>visit</u> them to look around and <u>interview people</u> — include notes you make on visits in your portfolio.

2) You need to describe the <u>main features</u> of ICT use by each of the organisations. Make sure you cover the following main <u>uses</u> of ICT in your descriptions:
   • How ICT is used to <u>store</u> information.
   • How ICT is used to <u>communicate</u> — between departments and with customers, suppliers, etc.
   • How ICT is used to carry out the <u>main work</u> of the organisation.

3) Give details of the <u>information used</u> by the ICT systems and the <u>processing</u> that takes place.

4) Describe at least two <u>advantages</u> and two <u>disadvantages</u> of the ICT systems used.

5) Comment on the <u>impact</u> that ICT has had on each organisation. Include changes in <u>working practices</u>, <u>costs</u> and <u>efficiency</u>.

HOW TO GET THE BEST MARKS:

1) Don't just describe how ICT is used — <u>analyse</u> and <u>evaluate</u> how well it meets the needs of each organisation, and the impact that it's had.

2) Mention the <u>security of data</u>, and how <u>robust</u> and <u>reliable</u> the systems used are.

3) Use three different <u>sources of information</u> in your report — e.g. your observations from visits to the organisations, interviews with staff, business documents used by the organisations, company websites, etc. Show that you've <u>verified</u> some of your sources (see p. 103).

Task 2 — Report on the Main Hardware Components of an ICT System

WORTH UP TO 18 MARKS

WHAT YOU NEED TO DO:

1) Describe the <u>hardware</u> used in one of the ICT systems from Task 1.

2) You need to describe <u>one</u> piece of hardware from <u>each</u> of the following five groups:
   • <u>input</u> devices   • <u>output</u> devices
   • <u>storage</u> devices   • <u>ports</u> and <u>cables</u>
   • <u>processing</u> devices

3) Explain how the different components in the system are <u>connected</u>.

HOW TO GET THE BEST MARKS:

1) Include lots of <u>specific detail</u> in your descriptions — like specifications, speeds, amount of memory and storage space, etc.

Finding out about hardware was another of Bob's favourites

2) Talk about the <u>cost</u> of the hardware — of individual components and the system as a whole.

3) Comment on how <u>efficient</u> the systems are. If you want to really impress, you could even suggest <u>alternative</u> hardware that might meet the needs of the organisation better.

Unit 2 Assessment Advice (AQA)

The <u>second two</u> tasks involve creating your <u>own ICT system</u>.

Task 3 — Design and Create a New ICT System

WORTH UP TO 35 MARKS

WHAT YOU NEED TO DO:

1) Identify the problem that your system is going to <u>solve</u>. You could design a system for a real organisation (perhaps one of the ones you looked at for tasks 1 and 2), e.g. to <u>replace</u> a manual system or <u>improve</u> an existing ICT system. Or you could design your system for a made-up purpose invented by you or your teacher.

2) The system you design <u>doesn't</u> have to be too complicated — they're not asking you to build a new type of computer or anything like that. For example, you could create a new <u>spreadsheet system</u> to help a company manage its stock, or a new <u>database</u> and <u>mail-merge</u> system to manage customer records and send out reminder letters.

3) Find out what your <u>users</u> will need the new system to do. You'll need to make a list of the <u>user requirements</u> and <u>explain</u> why each is needed.

4) When you know what's required, you can start planning the project. Ask yourself:

> - what are the objectives for the system?
> - what data types will be used?
> - what order should the tasks happen in?
> - what hardware will the system need?
> - what data will I need to collect?
> - what are the tasks that need to be done?
> - which software will I use and why?
> - what will the user need to do?

5) Produce a <u>design specification</u>. This should be a detailed description of the design for the ICT system. In it you must specify <u>information sources</u> for the system (including <u>data types</u>), <u>input</u>, <u>process</u> and <u>output</u> requirements, and the type of <u>application software</u> needed. Also comment on the <u>purpose</u> and <u>benefits</u> of the system.

6) Represent the system graphically. This just means draw a <u>data flow diagram</u> to give an overview of your new system, and to show how the information will flow through it.

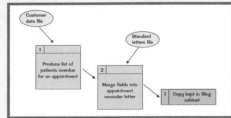

7) Next you'll have to actually <u>set up</u> the system. Show <u>evidence</u> of how you did this, stage by stage. Screen shots of it being developed and used are good for this.

A dataflow diagram (see p.64)

HOW TO GET THE BEST MARKS:

1) Choose a problem that requires a <u>complex solution</u> — e.g. a relational database or a spreadsheet with linked sheets.

2) Include a written <u>development diary</u> (see page 65) to go with your screen-shots showing the system being developed and used. This should <u>describe and explain</u> what's going on in each screen shot, and explain to the reader how you developed your system stage by stage.

3) Include in your commentary a description of the '<u>success factors</u>' of your system — what it's supposed to do at each stage for it to be effective in doing the job you designed it for.

4) Use <u>large data sets</u> when you're showing how your system works. E.g. if it's a new database of customer information, it should have <u>at least 25 records</u> in it, not just one or two. Include both <u>typical</u> and <u>erroneous</u> (wrong) data too, to show how your system responds.

> They think it's all over... it's not — turn over the page for the <u>last task</u> of Unit 2.

Unit 2 Assessment Advice (AQA)

Task 4 — Evaluate and Test Your New ICT System

WORTH UP TO 24 MARKS

WHAT YOU NEED TO DO:

1) <u>Test</u> your system. Use a range of data and test against <u>all</u> likely initial conditions.

2) You should test your system using <u>normal</u>, <u>invalid</u> and <u>extreme</u> data (see page 65).

3) Produce systematic <u>documentation</u> of the <u>results</u> of all your tests.

4) Use the results of your tests to <u>evaluate</u> your system — say how well it did its intended job. Comment on its <u>efficiency</u> and how <u>robust</u> it is (if it crashes or goes wrong a lot, its not very robust).

5) Use your tests to <u>refine</u> your system (make it work better). Provide <u>evidence</u> of any <u>improvements</u> you made following testing and explain them.

6) Produce a <u>user guide</u> to show other people how to use your system. You could do this as a booklet or as online help. You might use <u>screen images</u> to help you explain how to do the various tasks. It should be thorough enough that even people with only basic ICT knowledge will be able to use your system.

HOW TO GET THE BEST MARKS:

1) For high marks your evaluation should be really detailed and include evidence of evaluation by a <u>third party</u>. So basically you get someone else to try out your system and find out what they thought. Ideally this person should be qualified in some way — e.g. if you've produced a system for a real organisation, get someone from the organisation to try it out and give you feedback. Include this in your portfolio.

2) Evaluate your <u>user documentation</u>. Again, get <u>someone else</u> to try using it and ask them to give you feedback.

3) If possible, use this third party feedback to <u>improve</u> your system further. At least comment on what the person has said — if you're not going to change your system according to their suggestions, <u>say why</u>.

Doug hovered anxiously as he awaited Doreen's feedback.

Still no exam... but another 20 pages of A4... yay?

Hmmm, this 'no exam' lark might not be all it's cracked up to be. Seems like a lot of work. But on the other hand, if you put a bit of <u>effort</u> in, you've got all the time you need to <u>make sure</u> you end up with something really good that'll get you <u>top marks</u>. So it's all worth it. Happy ending.

Unit 3 Assessment Advice (AQA)

Unit 3 is also assessed using a portfolio of work marked out of 100. But it's a bit different to the other two Units because you'll have a limited time to complete the work, and you'll have to do it during 'controlled lessons' that'll be supervised.

You'll Be Given a Candidate's Booklet Before the Controlled Lessons Start

1) You have to do three tasks for Unit Three. Although the tasks are similar every year, the areas of society you have to write about and the intended audience may change. These will be described in detail in the Candidate's Booklet.

2) Read the Booklet carefully as soon as you get it — there's a lot of preparation you need to do before you turn up to your first controlled lesson. The Booklet isn't just a list of instructions and tasks, it's a valuable resource — it gives you ideas for the kind of research you should be doing, lists of everything you need to hand in, and a full mark breakdown for each task with advice on how to increase the marks awarded to you.

3) Ask your teacher to explain if there's something in the Booklet that you don't understand.

You'll Work on the Three Tasks During Controlled Lessons

1) This is when you'll do the actual work. You're entitled to a minimum of 10 hours and a maximum of 20 hours controlled lesson time — the actual amount's up to your teacher. You'll probably just have controlled lesson time instead of normal ICT lessons for a few weeks.

2) You can't do any research towards your tasks during controlled lesson time — this must all be done in your own time or during normal ICT lessons. You can't use the Internet or textbooks in controlled lessons, but you can take in your own research notes.

3) You can't work on the tasks themselves outside controlled lesson time, although you can do as much research then as you like. Your actual assessed work is all done on computer during controlled lessons, and saved there until you print it out at the end.

4) There won't be full exam conditions in controlled lessons, but you'll be supervised to make sure all work's your own. Finished work is sent to an AQA examiner to be marked — it's not marked by your teacher.

SOME TIPS ON DOING YOUR RESEARCH...

1) Start your research as soon as you get the Candidate's Booklet. It'll tell you the topic for each task, and give you ideas on what you need to find out about.

2) As part of your research you can interview people, observe ICT systems being used, or develop questionnaires and analyse the responses.

3) Use books, magazines, newspapers, websites, etc. Do Internet searches and provide evidence of this by printing out the queries you put into the search engine and the resulting list of links.

4) You need to include a List of Sources for each of the three tasks. You can do them in your own time, but they're an important part of the tasks (worth up to 8 marks per task) and must be handed in. In each List of Sources include every information source you used when researching the task — even people who helped you (apart from your teacher). Comment on how useful each source in the list was, and explain how you checked its accuracy.

Now turn over the page for some splendid advice on the actual tasks you'll need to do.

Unit 3 Assessment Advice (AQA)

Task 1 — Write a Report Describing Various Types of Technology

WORTH UP TO 30 MARKS

WHAT YOU NEED TO DO:

1) It's likely that you'll need to describe the different kinds of technology available to access and exchange information and carry out transactions within a particular area of society. For example, in 2003 students had to write about the Entertainment and Leisure area of society.

2) Look at examples from a range of technologies. For each one, explain the purpose and the main advantages and disadvantages. Look in the Candidate's Booklet — it'll tell you in detail what to cover.

HOW TO GET THE BEST MARKS:

1) Review the trends in technology over time, including likely future developments.

2) Show that you've used ICT tools to search for, select and organise the information.

Look back to page 103 for more detail on how to do this.

Task 2 — Create a Presentation on the Impact of ICT Developments

WORTH UP TO 52 MARKS

WHAT YOU NEED TO DO:

1) This will also focus on a particular area of society, which you'll be given in the Candidate's Booklet. In 2003 the area of society was Businesses and Organisations.

2) The presentation should be in the form of a computer slide show or a set of web pages. Use the features of the software you're using as fully as possible.

3) Describe the groups or individuals affected by ICT in this area of society, the needs it meets, the benefits of using it and the consequences for groups and individuals with restricted ICT access.

HOW TO GET THE BEST MARKS:

1) Suggest what effect future developments in ICT technology might have, and explore the ethical and moral implications of having access (or not having access) to ICT.

2) Make sure your presentation's appropriate for your audience, and say who this is.

3) Show that you've used ICT tools to search for, select and organise the information.

4) Write a short evaluation of your work to hand in too. How could it have been improved?

Task 3 — Make a Newsletter or Brochure About ICT Legislation

WORTH UP TO 18 MARKS

WHAT YOU NEED TO DO:

1) Outline the main purposes of ICT legislation, covering using ICT at work and at home. The Candidate's Booklet will tell you who your newsletter or brochure should be designed for and what to include.

2) Explain why each law was introduced, who it affects, and what type of ICT use is involved.

HOW TO GET THE BEST MARKS:

1) Explain how each law actually affects different organisations and other ICT users.

2) Produce an evaluation of your work. Comment on the layout and design, as well as the content.

And please please PLEASE always always ALWAYS...

...include a List of Sources for each task. It's just chucking marks away if you don't. Don't try to remember them all at the end, you won't be able to — keep a list as you work through the tasks.

Unit 1 Assessment Advice (OCR)

If your exam board is OCR, you'll be taking a <u>written exam</u> in either January or June. Dah dah DAH!
It's worth <u>one third</u> of your final marks, so you need to be <u>well prepared</u>. Read on...

Your OCR course is split into <u>three modules</u>, A, B and C (sections 1, 2 and 3 in this book).
<u>All 3 modules</u> are covered in the written exam. Luckily <u>only certain things</u> from each module
can be tested on the written paper, and I know what they are...

Here's What Could Be on the Exam From <u>Module A</u>

WHAT YOU NEED TO KNOW:

1) Presentation of information using <u>word-processing</u>, <u>desk-top publishing</u> and <u>multimedia presentation</u> software.

2) Use of <u>spreadsheet</u> software to organise and analyse numerical data.

3) Use of <u>database</u> software to organise and analyse structured information.

4) Use of the following applications by organisations:
   * applications that capture, manipulate and enhance <u>graphic images</u>.
   * applications that automate and control processes, like <u>CAD/CAM</u>.
   * applications that monitor and record <u>physical and environmental data</u>.
   You also need to be able to identify why a type of application is appropriate for an organisation's purposes, and the tools and facilities that make it appropriate.

5) <u>Standard ways of working</u> — this is to do with how to keep your work safe and confidential.

WHICH PAGES TO LEARN:

* **Section 1.1**
* **Pages 33–35**
* **Section 1.2**
* **Pages 39–40**

Have a look at page 103 too — this is an AQA advice page, but it has more on what exam boards mean by standard ways of working.

Here's What Could Be on the Exam From <u>Module B</u>

WHAT YOU NEED TO KNOW:

1) The four main <u>departments</u> found in an organisation:
   * sales
   * finance
   * purchasing
   * operations

2) The main <u>hardware</u> used in an ICT system:
   * input devices
   * processing devices
   * ports and cables
   * network protocols and services
   * output devices
   * storage devices
   * NICs, modems and ASDLs
   You'll also need to know <u>why</u> each device is used.

WHICH PAGES TO LEARN:

* **Section 2.1**
* **Section 2.2**

You don't need to know all the details for this, just an overview of what each department does.

TIP: Don't just learn <u>parrot fashion</u> — some questions test your <u>understanding</u> too.

<u>Turn over</u> for the next page of advice for Unit 1.

Unit 1 Assessment Advice (OCR)

Here's What Could Be on the Exam From Module C

WHAT YOU NEED TO KNOW:

1) <u>Internet</u> technologies (e.g. e-mail, the world wide web, multimedia, encryption).

2) Internet <u>connections</u> (e.g. modem, ISDN, ASDL, broadband).

3) <u>Mobile phone</u> technologies (e.g. SMS, WAP).

4) Digital <u>broadcasting</u>.

5) <u>PDAs</u> and Organisers.

6) Types of <u>storage</u> (e.g. DVD, minidisk).

7) <u>Touch-screen</u> technologies.

8) The <u>Data Protection</u> Act.

9) The <u>Copyright, Designs and Patents</u> Act.

10) The <u>Computer Misuse</u> Act.

11) The <u>Health and Safety at Work</u> Act.

12) <u>Health and Safety</u> Regulations.

13) The Regulation of <u>Investigatory Powers</u> Act.

13) ICT <u>fraud</u> and misuse of personal information.

14) Problems with <u>spam</u>, <u>chatrooms</u> and <u>viruses</u>.

WHICH PAGES TO LEARN:

- Pages 27
- Pages 78–80
- Pages 84–88

So there you go — those are the pages you'll need to <u>revise</u> to pass this exam.
If you've got all the stuff on them <u>committed to memory</u>, you should be fine.

Practising Past Papers is a Good Way to Improve

The exam lasts an <u>hour and a half</u>, and will include a variety of question types. These range from questions requiring <u>one word answers</u> to questions needing <u>longer written explanations</u>. Here's a <u>typical OCR exam question</u>:

"List four types of backing storage that a manufacturing company could use.
State the main use of each."

Nothing you can't handle if you know your stuff. That's why <u>learning the facts</u> is your main priority, but one other thing you can do that can make a big difference is to practise some <u>past papers</u>. Ask your teacher or tutor for some past papers, or have a look on <u>OCR's website</u>.

Bear in mind these general <u>exam tips</u> too:

- Read <u>everything carefully</u> — instructions on the front and the questions.
- Use the <u>marks allocated</u> to each question to decide how long and how detailed your answer should be.
- If you can't think of an answer, <u>move on</u> — you can always go back to it.
- Use <u>all the time</u> you've been given. If you finish early, check back through <u>your answers</u>.

Think of something calm.

Yippee! Just what you always wanted — an exam!

OK, I'm fooling no-one. Very few people love exams, but you can make them <u>much</u> more bearable by being <u>well prepared</u>. Then you'll have nothing to be scared of. So get <u>revising</u> those pages.

Unit 2 Assessment Advice (OCR)

The next 4 pages are about your Unit 2 <u>Business Systems Portfolio</u>. Your work for this will involve investigating <u>two organisations</u>' use of ICT, producing <u>documents</u> for them, and also producing a <u>new ICT system</u> for one of them. The Portfolio will be marked out of <u>50</u>.

Task a — A Report on How and Why Two Organisations Use ICT Systems

WORTH UP TO 8 MARKS

WHAT YOU NEED TO DO:

1) Choose two <u>quite different</u> organisations to study — ideally a small one that makes only limited use of ICT, and a big one that relies on ICT a lot. You could find them yourself, e.g. through a family member or part-time job, but check with your teacher that they're OK.

2) Visit the organisations, if possible, to see the systems being used and to talk to staff.

3) <u>Describe</u> in your report <u>how</u> the organisations use ICT. Think about things like:
   - What ICT is used for
   - the hardware used
   - the information needed for each system
   - the application software used

HOW TO GET THE BEST MARKS:

1) Don't just say how the organisations use ICT, say <u>why</u>.

2) Explain how the hardware and software used <u>meet the organisations' needs</u> and help them to communicate and function effectively.

Task b — A Report on the Documents used By the Organisations

WORTH UP TO 6 MARKS

WHAT YOU NEED TO DO:

1) Collect a <u>range</u> of documents from the two organisations. Try to get a <u>full range</u> — business letters, memos, flyers, invoices, newsletters, and presentations... and a load more besides.

2) Try to collect <u>similar</u> documents from both the organisations.

3) In your report, describe the <u>content</u> and <u>layout</u> of the documents the organisations use. Mention things like:

> key features of the documents, features that similar documents have in common, layout features (columns, paragraphs...), numbered lists, bullets, tables, colour, pictures...

4) Identify the <u>purpose</u> and the <u>intended reader</u> of each document. Comment on how well the writing and presentation styles used meet the purpose. You could even suggest <u>improvements</u>.

HOW TO GET THE BEST MARKS:

1) Look at documents from <u>other</u> organisations, besides the two you've already studied.

2) Use documents from at least <u>three</u> different organisations to draw some conclusions about <u>general standards</u> expected in business documents. State clearly in your report what your conclusions are, and use them when you produce your <u>own documents</u> later on.

3) Remember to include <u>all</u> the documents you've studied in your portfolio — you'll lose a <u>lot</u> of marks if you don't, as the examiner won't be able to judge whether your opinions were valid.

Turn over for more advice on Unit 2.

Unit 2 Assessment Advice (OCR)

Task c — Create Your Own Business Documents

WORTH UP TO
9 MARKS

WHAT YOU NEED TO DO:

1) Produce <u>at least three</u> business documents for an organisation. You could re-design real business documents you've studied, create new documents for one of the organisations you've looked at, or invent a new business and produce your documents for that.

2) You need to use the following software:

<u>Wordprocessing software</u> — You could produce a <u>letter</u> to customers telling them about a new product, or a <u>report</u> for colleagues on the results of a market research survey.

<u>Desktop publishing software</u> — You could produce a <u>poster or flyer</u> to advertise a new product, or a <u>newsletter</u> for staff about what's going on in the company. Include pictures as well as text in both.

<u>Presentation software</u> — E.g. make a <u>presentation</u> to sell your company's products to customers, or to tell the company directors about the latest sales figures.

3) When you've finished a <u>first draft</u> of each of your documents, print it out and <u>annotate</u> it to show any changes you could make to improve it. Check carefully for errors too, and note these on your draft copy. Then make all the changes and print out the <u>new version</u> too.

HOW TO GET THE BEST MARKS:

1) Produce <u>complex</u> documents that make use of advanced software features — e.g. your letter could be a <u>form letter</u> that's <u>mail-merged</u> with a list of customers to produce a <u>mail shot</u>. Incorporate charts, tables and graphics into your documents, use headers and footers, bullet points, wrap text — anything to show you can use <u>lots</u> of the software's features to create complex documents.

2) For the top marks on your presentation, use 5 or 6 slides and include lots of fancy features like <u>navigation buttons</u>, <u>animations</u> and different types of <u>multimedia</u>.

3) Develop your own <u>house style</u> (see p12) and use it in all your documents.

4) Your documents must meet their intended <u>purpose</u> and be suitable for the intended readers.

Unit 2 Assessment Advice (OCR)

The last tasks involve creating a new ICT system for one of the organisations you've studied.

Tasks d, e, f — Design and Create a New ICT System

WORTH UP TO 16 MARKS

WHAT YOU NEED TO DO:

1) Identify the problem that your system is going to solve. You should design a system for one of the organisations you studied for the other tasks, e.g. to replace a manual system or improve an existing ICT system.

2) The system you design doesn't have to be too complicated — they're not asking you to build a new type of computer or anything like that. For example, you could create a new spreadsheet system to help a company manage its stock, or a new database system mail-merged with a standard letter to manage customer records and send out reminder letters.

3) Start by investigating how the information flows in the system. You'll need to find out:

- who sends information, who receives information
- what information is passed and how it's passed
- what information is stored and how and where it's stored

Draw a dataflow diagram (see p63) to show these information flows. This is worth 6 marks.

4) Produce a design specification for the system you'll develop. This is worth 4 marks. It should be a detailed description of the design for the ICT system. In it you must include:

- the user requirements
- the input, processing and outputs required
- the type(s) of applications software needed
- the information sources
- the hardware needed

Also comment on the purpose and benefits of the system.

5) Next you'll have to actually set up the system. This is worth 6 marks. You'll have to show evidence of the system being developed and used. Keep a written development diary (p.65) of the steps carried out and take screen-shots to show what you did. Also include in your records examples of the input data you use, and printouts of the output obtained.

HOW TO GET THE BEST MARKS:

1) Choose a problem that requires a complex solution involving more than one type of application — e.g. a database mail-merged with a form letter to send out reminders to customers.

2) Include a detailed plan for testing the system in your design specification. This should include details of the tests you plan to do to check the system works, and you can also say what results you'd expect to see if your system is working as planned.

3) For top marks, your design specification and development diary should be clear and detailed enough for someone else with basic ICT knowledge to recreate your system.

4) Remember, you're allowed to ask your teacher for help if you get stuck, but only do this if you need to. If your teacher has to give you loads of help, you can't get as many marks.

The show's not over till the portfolio sings — turn over the final page on Unit 2.

Unit 2 Assessment Advice (OCR)

Tasks g, h — Test Your New System and Produce User Documentation

WORTH UP TO 11 MARKS

WHAT YOU NEED TO DO:

1) <u>Test</u> your system. Use a range of data and test against <u>all</u> likely initial conditions.

2) Your tests should include <u>normal</u>, <u>abnormal</u> (invalid) and <u>extreme</u> data (see page 65).

3) Keep <u>records</u> of all tests you carry out. Include <u>screen prints</u>, the data you <u>input</u> and printouts of the <u>output</u> produced as evidence of how your system responded to the tests.

4) Use your tests to <u>refine</u> your system (make it work better). Provide <u>evidence</u> of any <u>improvements</u> you made following testing and explain them.

5) <u>Evaluate</u> your system — say how well it did its intended job. Comment on its <u>efficiency</u> and how <u>robust</u> it is (if it crashes or goes wrong a lot, its not very robust). Testing and evaluation together are worth <u>6 marks</u>.

6) Produce a <u>user guide</u> to show other people how to use your system. This is worth <u>5 marks</u>. You could do this as a <u>booklet</u> or as <u>online help</u>.

7) Make sure you include instructions on how to:

• open the software	• input data	• obtain output
• print the output	• save work	• exit the software

Just press control and C to copy highlighted data!

Or your user guide could be an animated talking penguin. If you're feeling really fancy.

HOW TO GET THE BEST MARKS:

1) For high marks, follow your <u>test plan</u> (see page 113) when testing your system.

2) You should include evidence that shows you tested your system thoroughly both as you were <u>implementing</u> it and <u>after</u> the system was completed.

3) If you find while you're testing your system that part of it doesn't work properly, <u>don't</u> try and cover it up. This is actually a chance to <u>impress</u> the marker. Include the usual screen shots and printouts in your portfolio, and <u>annotate</u> them to say what's going wrong, <u>why</u> this has happened, and what you'll do to <u>correct</u> it. Then modify your system accordingly and print out another lot of <u>evidence</u> to show it's working properly now.

4) Use lots of <u>screen shots</u> of menus, input screens and so on in your user guide to show clearly what users need to do. Annotate them with <u>clear instructions</u>.

5) Use clear and simple <u>language</u> throughout your user guide. Lots of technical language will <u>not</u> impress the marker here, because your user guide is supposed to be straightforward enough for <u>anyone</u> to use.

6) If you want to <u>really</u> show off, get someone else to try using your user guide and ask them to give you <u>feedback</u>. Ideally this would be someone from the organisation you've developed the system for. Include what they said in your portfolio and use it to <u>improve</u> your user guide if possible.

Well, at least it's not an exam...

Don't panic, once you get into it you'll be fine. The most <u>important</u> thing to remember is that the person marking your work <u>can't</u> give you marks for anything unless there's <u>paper evidence</u> of it in the portfolio. And no <u>random printouts</u> either please — explain what everything is and be organised.

Unit 3 Assessment Advice (OCR)

For Unit 3 you produce an ICT Survey Portfolio. There are two main parts to this. First you'll carry out a survey on how people use ICT, and use databases and spreadsheets to record and analyse the responses. Then you'll research and produce a presentation on the effects of developments in ICT.

Task 1 — Carry Out a Survey to Collect Data to Use

WHAT YOU NEED TO DO:

1) You need to collect information to put in your spreadsheet and database. A good way to do this is by carrying out a survey. Your survey should be about a topic you've covered in Module C — people's use of mobile phones or the Internet are good, because you can ask family and friends.

2) Decide what you want to find out — think of about five or six different things, e.g. who uses mobiles more, males or females? Younger or older people? How long each day? More at weekends? Then write a questionnaire to help you find out. Remember, you'll need some numerical data so you can do calculations in your spreadsheet.

3) Include a copy of your questionnaire in your portfolio. Then use it to carry out your survey.

HOW TO GET THE BEST MARKS:

You're not actually marked on your questionnaire, so you don't need hundreds of responses or a real in-depth set of questions. You're only given marks for what you do with the data you collect. So just collect enough to make sure you can do a good job with your database and spreadsheet.

Task 2 — Set Up a Database to Store and Process the Information

This task covers assessment point b of the specification.

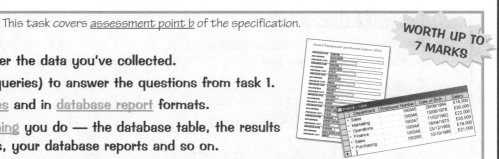

WORTH UP TO 7 MARKS

WHAT YOU NEED TO DO:

1) Set up a database and enter the data you've collected.

2) Sort and search it (using queries) to answer the questions from task 1.

3) Display the results as tables and in database report formats.

4) Print out copies of everything you do — the database table, the results of your sorts and searches, your database reports and so on.

5) Annotate your printouts to show what you did. Explain why you did it — what were you trying to find out, and what result did you get? Put them in your portfolio.

HOW TO GET THE BEST MARKS:

1) Your database must have at least two related tables. (Look back at Section 1.2 to remind yourself about harder database and spreadsheet stuff. Or you could use the 'Help' function in the software.)

2) Do complex queries (using 'AND' and 'OR') to help you analyse the data in your database.

3) For the best grades, create forms for data input and set up validation rules for different types of data.

4) You must also customise the format of the database reports you produce so that they're suited to their purpose and audience.

5) And for goodness' sake, if you're going to bother doing all this flashy stuff, make sure the examiner knows it. You'll have to have paper copies which prove that you've done all these things, and they need to be annotated so you can say what you've done, how and why.

Turn over for more help on Unit 3.

Unit 3 Assessment Advice (OCR)

Task 3 — Set Up a Spreadsheet to Store and Process the Information

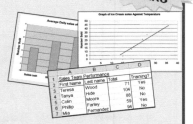

WORTH UP TO 7 MARKS

WHAT YOU NEED TO DO:
This task covers assessment point c of the specification.

1) Set up a spreadsheet and enter some of your data.

2) Format the data. Use suitable titles and row and column headings.

3) Enter formulae to calculate results to some of the questions from task 1.

4) Copy formulae down columns or across rows as necessary.
Move data between cells, and insert and delete rows and columns.

5) Produce graphs and charts to help you display your results. Use suitable titles and labels.

6) Make print-outs to show everything you do. Annotate them and include them in your portfolio.

HOW TO GET THE BEST MARKS:

1) Your spreadsheet should be quite complex, using functions like SUM and AVERAGE.

2) Use absolute cell references, and do some print-outs of specific areas of the spreadsheet.

3) Combine sections of your spreadsheet with charts and graphs in a report.

4) Like with the database work, print out clear evidence that you've done all this stuff.

Task 4 — Research into the Effects of ICT Developments

WORTH UP TO 7 MARKS

WHAT YOU NEED TO DO:
This task covers assessment point a of the specification.

1) Research the effects of ICT developments (so you can use the information in
a presentation — see next page). Your research must cover the impact of ICT on:
- business
- working styles and employment opportunities
- personal communication
- community activities
- people with special/particular needs

TIP: keep printouts, notes, cuttings and copies of the info you find

2) Identify and use a variety of resources, including the Internet, books, ICT magazines, newspapers
(many have weekly supplements on ICT developments) and TV and radio programmes. You could
visit organisations that use new technologies and interview people — maybe some older people
to find out what it was like before technologies you're used to became widespread.

HOW TO GET THE BEST MARKS:

1) Include a full bibliography listing every source of information you've used. This includes people
(give their name and role), web sites (give the web address), newspapers (title and date) and
programmes (name, channel and date).

2) Show you've used advanced search techniques on the Internet. Use bookmarks and favourites.

3) Where possible, find information on a topic from more than one source so you can compare them
and make sure the information is accurate.

4) For the best marks, you've got to use resources of all types and be selective
— only use the most relevant and appropriate bits from the information you find.

Unit 3 Assessment Advice (OCR)

The last part of Unit 3 involves turning what you've learned about the effects of ICT into a presentation.

Task 5 — Create a Multimedia Presentation on the Impact of ICT

WORTH UP TO 29 MARKS

This task covers assessment points d, e, f and g of the specification.

For this task you need to look at the impact of ICT in these 5 key areas:

- business
- working styles and employment opportunities
- personal communication
- community activities
- people with special/particular needs

WHAT YOU NEED TO DO:

1) For each of the five areas above...
Consider at least four different people or groups of people and explain how ICT developments would affect them.

E.g. for "people with particular needs", you could look at these four groups: people with poor vision, hearing difficulties, limited movement and learning difficulties.

2) For each of the five areas above...
— Explain in detail two needs that can met by using ICT.
— Explain in detail two benefits of using ICT.

3) For each of the five areas above...
Consider people who have restricted or no access to ICT. Explain how this would affect them.

You need to present some of this information as a multimedia presentation. You don't have to cover all the stuff above in your presentation, but you should cover a big chunk of it. Any stuff above that you haven't put in your presentation should go in a word-processed report to be included in your portfolio.

HOW TO GET THE BEST MARKS:

1) The three tasks above are worth 7, 7 and 6 marks respectively.
If you want to get high marks, you need to:

- do everything we've said above, even though it seems like a lot — if you don't write about four different groups for task 1 above, you can't get full marks. It's as simple as that.

- explain things in detail to show that you've really thought about it properly.

2) As well as getting marks for what you write, there's also 9 marks available for actually creating the presentation. If you want to get all of these you need to make sure that your presentation is really good and quite complex. Here's some tips for doing this...

- Use lots of slides — you won't get high marks if you only use 2 slides.

- Use a structure diagram or storyboard to plan your presentation (stick it in your portfolio).

- The presentation should be interactive and allow the user to take different paths through it.

- It should use many types of media, e.g. text, images, sounds, animations, videos. Create and edit some multimedia elements yourself. Use appropriate software to edit the multimedia components.

So that'll take you, what? About twenty minutes...?

Blimey, that's quite a bit of work. You've got to carry out a survey. You've got to use database, spreadsheet and presentation software. You've got to do loads of research, and you've got to write good material for your presentation. Don't be overwhelmed though — just get started. Right now.

Final Tips for Producing Portfolios

Your teacher will probably have been telling you all this stuff until they're <u>blue in the face</u>. But just to make sure they haven't been wasting their breath, here's a little <u>list</u> of the things you <u>must</u> remember when you're putting portfolios together.

You'll need a Portfolio for each Coursework Unit

To start with, a few basic (but important) points about your portfolios...

1) You'll have to produce a portfolio for each of your <u>coursework units</u>. If you're doing AQA, you'll need to do one for all 3 units.

2) In the coursework units, there's various <u>tasks</u> you'll need to do. All these separate pieces of work go together to make your portfolio.

3) The portfolios are marked by your <u>teacher</u> and moderated by the exam board (except AQA unit 3 which is marked externally).

4) The portfolios make up <u>two thirds</u> (or <u>all</u> for AQA) of your final grade, so they're pretty important...

Your Portfolios Should Contain Only Your Best Work

As you're working through your Applied ICT course, by all means keep <u>all</u> your work — assignment work, notes from your lessons, exercises you've done in class — in a folder. This is sensible, as you'll have it all in the one place and you <u>won't lose anything</u>.

But remember...

- this is <u>not</u> a portfolio, and the marker will not be at all impressed if you call it one and hand it in.

- Your portfolios should be <u>well-organised</u>, <u>well-structured</u> and tailored <u>exactly</u> to the requirements of each of the assignments in them.

- There should be no notes from lessons, no random print-outs, nothing but your <u>best work</u>, all fitting clearly together.

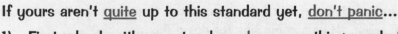

If yours aren't <u>quite</u> up to this standard yet, <u>don't panic</u>...

1) First, check with your teacher <u>when</u> everything needs to be handed in — the last thing you want is to <u>run out of time</u>.

2) Make sure you've got all the work that you've done for each assignment back from them if they've been looking after it. And ask them which <u>exam board</u> you're doing.

3) Now study the <u>assessment advice</u> for <u>your</u> exam board in this book (if you haven't already). You'll find details of all the stuff you should have done for each <u>assignment</u> in each <u>Unit</u>, and you can use this to start getting your work into some kind of <u>order</u>.

4) Make sure you haven't <u>missed anything out</u>, and get it added in <u>quick</u> if you have.

exam bored

Final Tips for Producing Portfolios

Make Your Portfolios Easy to Follow

1) You can make your work look more professional and help it all hang together by using <u>headers and footers</u> throughout. These could show your name, candidate number (when you know it) and the course title (GCSE Applied ICT). But <u>don't</u> number the pages in your assignments yet — you'll need to add page numbers for the <u>whole portfolio</u> later on.

2) We all like an easy life and that includes your marker. Make it easy for them to give you marks by using <u>helpful headings</u> in your work, so they can see what you've done straight away. Suppose you've asked others for their opinion about your work as part of your evaluation, because you know your exam board awards more marks if you do. Well, put in a <u>subheading</u> in your evaluation: "What other people think". Bingo — <u>more marks</u>.

3) When you do <u>print-outs</u> from your project (of spreadsheets, databases, etc.) <u>annotate</u> them to explain what you've done. Do this <u>in pen</u> — it takes ages on the computer and <u>doesn't</u> get you more marks.

4) This last tip is just for <u>spreadsheets</u>. You'll need to provide <u>two copies</u> of most of your spreadsheets. One should show the 'ordinary' spreadsheet, and the other one should show the <u>formulas</u> with row and column headings and a grid. Ask your teacher how to do this. Make sure you annotate <u>both</u> prints. This may seem like a hassle, but the marker won't have evidence of how you've been <u>using your spreadsheets</u> if you don't do both prints.

Warning — Make Sure it's All Your Own Work

1) Make sure there's nobody else's work in with yours. <u>I</u> know you're honest, but the exam boards take a very dim view of two candidates' work being <u>too similar</u>. If they're feeling mean (and that <u>is</u> their natural state), you may get <u>no GCSEs at all</u> if they think you've cheated.

2) There's one <u>exception</u> to that. If you've done a <u>joint project</u>, you must <u>annotate</u> the work clearly to show whose work is whose.

3) You'll need to include bits in your work that come from <u>books</u> or <u>websites</u>. That's fine, but you must <u>reference</u> these — which just means that you say where it's come from. You might get more marks for saying (with reasons) how <u>reliable</u> you think it is. References can go either next to the chunk you've 'borrowed', or at the end of the assignment.

Final Tips for Producing Portfolios

And Last of All — Sort Out the Presentation

OK so it's not as important as the actual <u>quality</u> of your work — but these little tricks <u>can</u> help grab you a couple of extra marks. Markers are shallow like that, no matter how much they deny it.

Do this stuff at the <u>very end</u>:

1) Make a <u>front cover</u>. On it you should have:
   • your <u>name</u> and <u>candidate number</u>
   • the course name ("<u>GCSE Applied ICT</u>")
   • the <u>unit number</u>
   • your school or college's <u>centre name</u> and <u>centre number</u>. Ask your teacher or tutor if you don't know any of these.

2) Separate the different assignments with <u>heading pages</u>. These don't have to be complicated — just put the name of the assignment on them.

3) <u>Number</u> your pages. The first page after the front cover should be page 1, and then just number <u>right through</u> until the last page. Don't do weird numberings like "Section 3b, part a, page 9". This just confuses the poor old marker.

4) Include a <u>contents page</u>, with all your main titles and their page numbers. This makes life easier for the marker and puts them in a happy mood, which has got to be good news.

5) Hold it all together in a <u>simple binder</u>.

<u>A good way to organise a portfolio</u>

1) Front cover

2) Contents page

3) Marking sheet
   (possibly — ask your teacher)

4) Declaration sheet
   (possibly — ask your teacher)

5) Brief for first task,
   or divider with task title

6) First task

7) Brief for second task,
   or divider with task title

8) Second task

...and so on.

And that's it. Portfolio done. Yep, thought you'd be pleased.

Ding dong — the portfolio's gone...

The successful completion of a portfolio brings all sorts of different people <u>together</u> in celebration. Babies, skiers, jumping teenagers in pipes, odd waving women... they're all delighted. So let's not disappoint them. One <u>final effort</u>, and then the blasted thing will be out of your life <u>forever</u>.

Index

Index

Index

mouse 48
moving text 1
MP3 87
multi-part stationery 53
multimedia 15
multimedia encyclopaedias 92
my girlfriend 52
my mate Andy 31

N

National Insurance 45
navigation (presentations) 15
network 40, 54, 58, 71
network interface card (NIC) 58
network managers 75
network protocols 58
network technician 71
newsletter design 12
newspaper 46
NHS Direct 88
NOT 24
noticeboard 10
nozzles 53
numbering in text 2

O

object-based graphics software 7
objectives 61
obsolete 66
OCR (Optical Character Recognition) 49
office jobs 75
OMR (Optical Mark Recognition) 49
on-line box offices 50
online auctions 68
online discussions 88
online services 68 – 70
online shopping 68
operating system 55
operations department 46
optical disks 57
ordering goods 44
organisation needs 42
orphans 3
outdoor activities 89
output devices 52
output screens 62

P

page printers 53
page set up 3
painting software 7
parallel implementation 66
parallel port 54
passwords 40
paste 1
patient records 64

pay per view 85
paying bills 82
payroll system 45
performance criteria 61
peripherals 54
permanent hard copy 53
permanent memory 55
Personal Digital Assistants (PDAs) 87
phased implementation 66
photo-editing software 9, 50
physical security 40
pie charts 22
pimples (laptops) 48
pixels 7, 50, 52
plug-ins 27
pop-up adverts 73
portals 28
portfolio advice 118 – 120
    Edexcel 96 – 100
    AQA 101 – 108
    OCR 111 – 117
portrait 3
ports 54
Powerpoint 15
presentations 13 – 16, 38
pressure groups 83
printers 53
printhead 53
prison 78
processing power 55
producing a newspaper 12
programmers 75
publishing software 10
purchasing department 44

Q

questionnaire 37
quiz machines in pubs 50
QWERTY keyboards 48

R

RAM (Random-Access Memory) 55
read-only 40
read/write head 56
Regulations of Investigatory Powers Act (2000) 79
relational databases 23
repetitive strain injury (RSI) 39
resizing objects 8
resolution 7
robots 46, 49
ROM (Read-Only Memory) 55
Ronan Keating 28
rotating objects 8
route planning software 89
routine operations 5

S

SADFLAB 40
sales department 43
satellite dish 85
satellites 89
saving your work 55
scanners 7, 49
scatter graphs 22
schools 92
script 16
searching databases 24
searching the Internet 28
secondary storage 56
security 40, 70
sensors 35, 48 – 50
sensory impairments 90
sequential access 57
serial access 57
serial numbers 40
serial ports 54
servo-motors 52
sharpness 9
shift key 1
shortcuts 1
single-line spacing 2
slide master 14
slides 13 – 16
snag 66
software piracy 78
somewhere over the rainbow 50
sound 52
spam 73, 80
spam e-mail 43
speakers 52
special effects 50
speech synthesis 52, 90
speed of an internet connection 27
spell-checking 4
spreadsheet 18, 45
    absolute cell reference 20
    cells 18
    conditional formatting 19
    coordinates 18
    formulas 20
    relative cell references 20
standard letter 6
standard ways of working 39 – 40, 103
stepper-motors 52
stock control 44
storage medium 40, 55 – 57, 64
streaming media 82
subtitles 90
supermarket 46
symbols 64
system flow charts 64
system life cycle 60
systems analysts 60, 75

Index

T

tables 3
talking computers 52
tax 45
technicians 75
telephone helplines 50
teleworking 76, 91
temperature sensors 50
template 5, 12
temporary memory 55
testing an IT system 65
text formatting 2
text messages 84
text size 2
text wrapping 11
Thumper 21
toner cartridge 53
top-down diagrams 63
touch screen terminals 50, 88
touch sensitive pads 48
touch-tone telephones 50
tourist office 88
tracker balls on laptops 48
traffic flow 35
training staff 77
transactions 43
travel information 89
triple click 1
trojans 71

U

unauthorised access 78
underlining 2
undo 1
Universal serial bus ports (USB) 54
unusual hobbies 83
upper limb disorder (ULD) 39
URL (Uniform Resource Locator) 28
user documentation 65
user friendly 62
user requirements 61

V

validation 19
VDU (Visual Display Unit) 52
vector-based software 7
verification 64
video cameras 50, 86
video digitisers 50
video recorder 57
video rental shop 42
virtual reality 86

viruses 31, 71, 78, 80
voice recognition software 50, 91
volatile memory 55

W

WAN (Wide Area Network) 27, 58
WAP mobile phone 31, 84
weather forecasts 35
web bots 30
web browser 27, 29
web pages 38
web site / web page
    28 – 30, 68 – 69, 71
widows 3
wizards 25
word count 5
word processing 1, 49
workload 66
workplace 75
WORM 57
wrapping text 11
writing style 12, 36
WWW (World Wide Web) 27

Z

ZIP disks 57